Mt. Rainier and the Nisqually Glacier

The National Parks of the Northwest

by Bob & Ira Spring
Text by Harvey Manning

Maps   Helen Sherman and Marge Mueller

 **Superior** PUBLISHING COMPANY
708 SIXTH AVE. NORTH, SEATTLE, WASH.

First edition

Library of Congress Cataloging in Publication Data

Spring, Robert, 1918-
National parks of the Northwest.

"A Salisbury Press book."
1. National parks and reserves—Northwest, Pacific
— Northwest, Pacific — Pictorial works.
2. Northwest, Pacific — Description and travel —
1951-
Views. I. Spring, Ira, joint author.
II. Manning, Harvey, joint author.
III. Title.
F852.2.S648 917.95'0022'2 76-6935
ISBN O-87564-015-X

Printed and bound in Canada

CONTENTS

Hikers on Cascade Pass. In distance, Eldorado Peak

INTRODUCTION: NATIONAL PARKS OF THE NORTHWEST

The 1872 creation of Yellowstone National Park, the world's first such preserve, in one respect was slightly premature—for some years visitors to the park, and the superintendent as well, on occasion were chased out by Indians. Over the next two decades, however, both the American Indian and the American frontier were rather thoroughly eliminated by the American pioneer, sourly characterized by Charlie Russell as a person who "destroys things and calls it civilization." Not every American deserved the condemnation. A few felt the need to balance exploitation with preservation and saw Yellowstone as their precedent. In 1890 granite canyons and sequoia groves of the Sierra Nevada were placed in national parks and the idea flared to a brightness inspiring citizens West and East.

Nowhere has the idea been more intimately interwoven with regional history than in the Pacific Northwest. The first park was close to the east in what is now Wyoming and the next ones not far to the south in California. Following them in 1899 was Mount Rainier National Park and in 1902 Crater Lake National Park.

As the frontier retreated into memory the idea flourished, but not without dissent; far from withering, the atavistic urge to "destroy and civilize" grew more and more virulent as there was less and less remaining undestroyed. Resistance to preservation became so bitter that not for 8 years had a new park been established in the West when, in 1938, the battle was won for Olympic National Park. After that, and the companion victory for Kings Canyon in the Sierra in 1940, a quarter-century passed in which the West obtained only one additional park entirely new, as distinguished from a change in name from an older protected status. Many a pundit pronounced the idea dead, confidently predicting there never would be another park in America. But in 1968 two of the longest and hardest-fought campaigns in the annals of the movement brought establishment of not one but two parks in the Northwest, Redwood and North Cascades, and so much for pundits.

An early fruit of the idea's renewed vigor was the decision by Congress in 1972 to study the Idaho Sawtooths for what would be that state's first national park. Impetus was strengthened for an Oregon Volcanoes National Park, centered on Mt. Jefferson and the Three Sisters, that would contain the most abundant and diverse examples of vulcanism in the nation. Proposals were put forth to enlarge to proper size Mount Rainier, Olympic, Redwood, and North Cascades National Parks.

Siblings of national parks and since 1933 administered by the National Park Service are the national monuments. Their enabling legislation, the Antiquities Act of 1906, rather narrowly intended by its framers to protect sites of exceptional historic or scientific importance, in a series of precedent-setting actions by President Theodore Roosevelt was given a very broad interpretation; for example, he established by proclamation a national monument in the Olympic Mountains three decades before creation of a national park there.

Presently-existing national monuments in the Northwest encompass the Lava Beds in northern California, Oregon Caves and John Day Fossil Beds in Oregon, Whitman Landmark (on the Oregon Trail) in Washington, and Craters of the Moon in Idaho. Being studied are the fossil beds near Hagerman, Idaho, on the Snake River, and the striking geologic formations of City of Rocks on the Idaho-Utah border. Citizen groups are urging monument status for two Cascade volcanoes, St. Helens in Washington and Shasta in California, and for the Columbia Gorge between Oregon and Washington.

Outside the scope of this book are still other units under jurisdiction of the National Park Service. The Fort Clatsop National Memorial at Astoria, Oregon, marks an encampment of the Lewis and Clark Expedition. The Fort Vancouver National Historic Site at Vancouver, Washington, contains the 1825-49 western headquarters of the Hudson's Bay Company, and the McLaughlin House National Historic Site at Oregon City, the home of the company's long-time regional chief, known as the "Father of Oregon." The San Juan National Historic Park on Washington's San Juan Island commemorates the "Pig War" of the 1860s which ended in settling the final segment of the boundary between the United States and Canada. Scattered through the region are a number of Natural Landmarks. The category of National Recreation Area is bewilderingly loose, no two being quite the same in purpose and administration—the Sawtooth National Recreation Area, for example, is under the U.S. Forest Service. Northwest areas of this name under the National Park Service are Coulee Dam, providing reservoir sport, and Ross Lake and Lake Chelan, administered with the North Cascades National Park.

If a traveler is confused by the variety of forms of protection given by the federal government, no wonder; over the years the protectionism movement has taken several crisscrossing but separate paths.

The national forests, administered by the U.S. Forest Service, a bureau of the Department of Agriculture, had their inception in the 1891 Forest Reserve Act which authorized presidents to withdraw forests and watersheds from private preemption under such land-giveaway legislation as the Homestead Act. The basic philosophy of the Forest Service is a utilitarian "conservation" for wise economic use; through most of their extent the forests are managed for simultaneous logging-mining-grazing-recreation-everything else, called "multiple use." However, in the 1920s the Forest Service began setting some lands aside from unrestricted exploitation, naming them "primitive areas"; subsequently these have been reclassified as "wildernesses" under terms of the 1964 Wilderness Act. Finally, Congress has created under the Forest Service a number of "national recreation areas," including not only the aforementioned Sawtooth but also Oregon Dunes and Hells Canyon; another is proposed for the Alpine Lakes section of the Washington Cascades.

Despite some overlaps and parallels, purposes of the U.S. Forest Service are distinct from those of the National Park Service, a bureau of the Department of the Interior. When previous haphazard administration of national parks was, in 1916, replaced by centralized control, the Act of Congress plainly spelled out the difference, directing the newly-founded Park Service "...to conserve the scenery and the natural and historic objects and the wild life therein and to provide for the enjoyment of same in such manner and by such means as will leave them unimpaired for future Americans."

The difference between national forest and national park may best be suggested by comparing the highest form of protection given in each, coverage by the Wilderness Act. In both forest and park a dedicated wilderness is an area where ". . . the earth and its community of life are untrammeled by man, where man himself is a visitor who does not remain . . ." However, in a forest wilderness grazing by cattle and sheep is permitted; not so in the wilderness or any other portion of a park. In a forest wilderness mining is permitted; not so in any part of a park, except where private holdings predate the park. Finally, in a forest wilderness hunting is allowed; not so anywhere in any parks of the Northwest, which thus are the region's only large gunfree refuges where entire populations of animals and birds live in a natural balance with each other and the land.

Two seasons at Big Meadow on Hurricane Ridge. Beyond the visitor center is the Bailey Range, topped by 6995-foot Mt. Carrie.

THE
OLYMPIC NATIONAL PARK

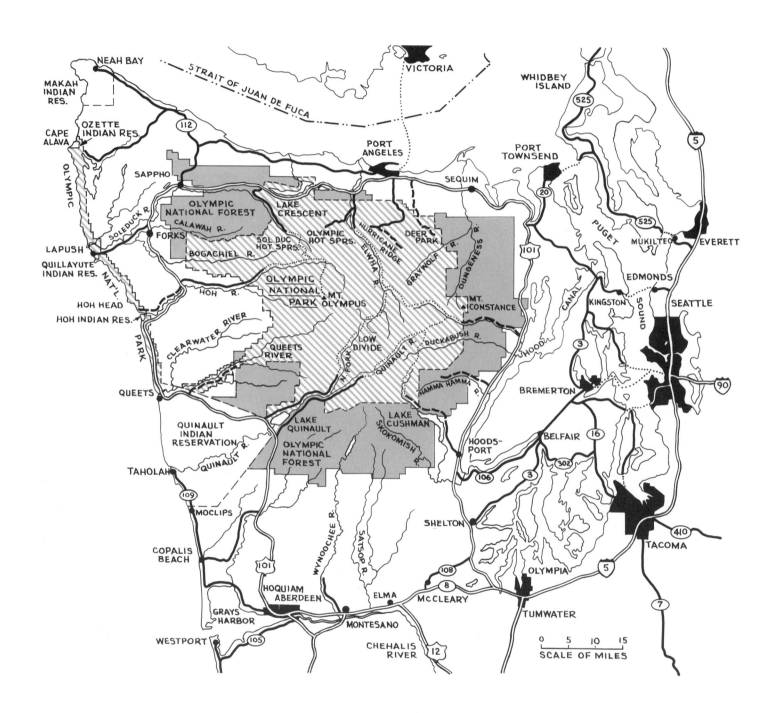

Previous page: Big Meadow and visitor center
on Hurricane Ridge. In background, the
Bailey Range, topped by 6995-foot Mount Carrie

10

OLYMPIC NATIONAL PARK

On a sunny day walk wet-bright sands by white explosions of breakers; pause now and then to watch bald eagles circling on high, gulls wheeling close above, cormorants and murres swimming and diving, sandpipers running. Return at night to see the moon's slow descent into the ocean and in darkness, beside the final wilderness, feel the rhythms of eternity. Return again — warily — during a winter storm, sideways-blasting rain so vicious eyes scarcely can open to glimpse gobs of spindrift ripped from wave crests and flung high and away, jumbles of driftwood logs hurled against spruce thickets in a terrible grinding thunder, and be frightened by surf ranking among the most violent anywhere on Earth.

Drive a short way inland to a valley road-end and enter the Olympic rain forest, described by the famous naturalist, Roger Tory Peterson, as "the greatest weight of living matter, per acre, in the world!" Far below crowns of tall spruce and hemlock, under maples swollen in trunk and branch with moss, amid seedlings and shrubs and ferns, listen to wind in treetops and to the river rushing down its sky-open avenue.

Backpack 2 days upward to alpine flower fields, step from gray moraine onto wide glacier, climb to the 7965-foot summit of Mount Olympus, so buried in ice it seems magically transported from Alaska, and if clouds allow, look 30 miles west over green waves of forest to the ocean.

Thus may one be properly introduced to the only surf-to-glacier national park in the conterminous 48 states and prepared for further wanderings.

Bounded on three sides by the Pacific Ocean, the Strait of Juan de Fuca, and fiord-like Hood Canal, the Olympic Peninsula rises gradually on south and west, abruptly on north and east, to the Olympic Mountains, not high compared to other ranges of the West but surpassed by few in tallness: Mount Constance stands 7743 feet above Hood Canal 10 miles distant, and Olympus 7500 feet above the Hoh River at its base.

Sitting squarely in the path of storms sweeping down from the Bering Sea (and even an occasional typhoon strayed north from the tropics), the west flanks are thoroughly drenched: average annual precipitation on the coast is 90 inches, at the Hoh Ranger Station 142 inches, and on Olympus 220 inches. When it's not raining it's generally fogging — during the ordinary year sunlight pokes into rain forest depths and brightens Olympus glaciers about one day in three. Yet 35 miles eastward the sun is no stranger; annual precipitation is a meager 15-20 inches in the rainshadow that extends along Hood Canal and out over Sequim prairies to the San Juan Islands.

Forming a rough square 40 miles on a side that encompasses about half the mountain range, with an additional 50-mile strip of ocean shore, the nearly 900,000 acres of Olympic National Park are for the most part little changed since the coming of man. Despite recurrent demands to "open up" the interior, the vision of the founders has not been betrayed and the park remains one of the nation's largest wildernesses.

A highway circles the park and stub roads push up a number of valleys and onto two ridges, allowing motorists to enjoy ocean, rain forest, and views of Olympus from blossom-bright alpine meadows — the three quintessential park experiences. However, no road crosses the range and the park's special glory is the back country, hikers' country, so vast that though rangers issue 100,000 camping permits a year, few trails are crowded and no ingenuity is required to gain solitude.

The spaciousness of the park and the freedom from machines also make it one of the continent's grandest wildlife sanctuaries, sufficiently large to hold thousands upon thousands of stay-at-home creatures as well as the full migratory range of animals which move seasonally from high to low. No tinkering is permitted with population dynamics by hunters; cougar and coyote and other predators thrive and therefore so do their prey, all living with each other and the land in a natural balance and harmony.

Footbridge over East Fork Quinault River

Ferry leaving Edmonds for Kingston. The skyline peaks are, left to right,
Washington (6255 feet), Stone (6612), twin summits of The Brothers (6866),
and Jupiter (5701).

Indians fishing at the mouth of the Quillayute River

HISTORY

For millenia the Olympic Peninsula has been inhabited, but until the past century solely at sealevel. The Indians of old had no good reason to venture far from the rich table spread by nature in tidal pools and rivermouths, though enough did there was a word for the occasional inland rover — a word translating as "fool." Many tribes called the shunned mountains "Home of the Thunderbird," the monster which caused commotions in the sky.

The first known sighting of the range by Europeans was in 1774, when Juan Perez, sailing offshore, called the highest point Santa Rosalia. The fur trade brought a rush of exploiters, one of whom, the Englishman John Meares, in 1788 renamed the peak Olympus, feeling if it weren't the home of the gods it should be. Having decimated the sea otter, whites paid little further attention to the peninsula. Only in the last decade of the 19th century was the interior explored, most notably by the Press Expedition (named for the sponsoring Seattle newspaper) in the winter-spring of 1889-90, the summer 1890 party led by Lieutenant Joseph O'Neil (first to call for a national park), and the U.S. Geological Survey mapmakers of 1898-1900. The first mass intrusion by non-professional explorers came in 1907 when the newly-organized Seattle-based club, The Mountaineers, made the initial ascent of Mount Olympus.

In 1897 President Cleveland established the Olympic Forest Reserve, from which, in 1906, President Roosevelt set aside the Mount Olympus National Monument to preserve the herds of elk being gang-slaughtered — not for their flesh but their teeth, then fashionable as watchfobs. After decades of controversy O'Neil was heeded and in 1938 another President Roosevelt signed the act placing the old monument and adjacent lands in the new Olympic National Park.

Repeated attempts have been defeated to reduce the size of the park, which has become increasingly valued with the advance of logging and roads everywhere else on the peninsula. Indeed, citizen groups now are seeking to add to the park the stretch of wild coast north to Point of Arches and Shi Shi Beach, establish a national seashore to protect portions of the Strait of Juan de Fuca and Hood Canal, and create park-adjoining wilderness areas in Olympic National Forest.

VISITOR FACILITIES

Highway 101, completed in 1930, encircles the Olympic Peninsula and links towns and resorts offering every variety of visitor services convenient to the park, which therefore is not called upon to provide within its boundaries extensive facilities of a highly "civilized" kind.

The highway is mere yards from the surf in the vicinity of Kalaloch, location of a lodge, visitor center, and campground. Sideroads lead to the ocean at LaPush (cabins, camping), Rialto Beach (visitor center and nearby campground), and within 3 miles by trail at Ozette Lake.

Dead-end roads ascend valleys to campgrounds in the park and the national forest: from Hood Canal, up the Skokomish, Hamma Hamma, Duckabush, Dosewallips, and Quilcene Rivers; from the Strait of Juan de Fuca, up the Dungeness and Elwha Rivers and to Heart of the Hills; and from the ocean, up the Soleduck, Bogachiel, Hoh, Queets, and Quinault Rivers.

The most popular valley is the Hoh, where the road-end visitor center gives a superb introduction to self-guiding nature trails starting at the door and proceeding into rain forest.

At park headquarters in Port Angeles the visitor center has Indian and geologic displays. Lake Crescent and Lake Quinault, both on the highway, offer camping, lodging, and boating.

The principal high-country access is the all-year surfaced road to 5225-foot Big Meadow on Hurricane Ridge, site of a visitor center and a winter ski area as much used for family play and tours on skis and snowshoes as for tow-hill running. A narrow dirt road continues along the ridge through more flowers and views to Obstruction Point. The meager road to 5400-foot Deer Park is steep, rough, and twisty, recommended only to the nerveless automobilist.

Several low-elevation campgrounds are open in winter, the most dramatic season at the ocean and in the opinion of philosophers the best time of year for profound thoughts while slowly walking rain-forest trails.

Lake Crescent and Mount Storm King, 4534 feet

Duckabush valley farm, now gone

Moss-covered vine maple in Hoh rain forest

Nurse log near Hoh River visitor center

Unfurling sword fern
Mossy log
Unfurling deer fern

RAIN FOREST

Nowhere else on Earth grow such forests as once were common all along the Pacific Northwest coast. Nowhere, now, do classic examples survive except in the park-protected valleys of the Hoh, Queets, and Quinault.

Their perfection here results from specific conditions: rainfall of up to 150 inches a year and, equally important, sea fogs seeping through the trees, providing a water-rich atmosphere the year around; temperatures only occasionally and briefly dipping below the high 40s and rising above the low 70s; and well-drained bottomlands, climax rain forest being restricted to alluvial flats under 1000 feet.

These conditions make the rain forest. What characteristics give the distinctive feel? For one, huge coniferous trees, many 700 years old, 12 feet in diameter, 300 feet tall. Sitka spruce and western hemlock dominate, Douglas-fir and western redcedar relatively few in numbers.

Beneath this high canopy is a billowing layer of deciduous trees, the bigleaf maple particularly striking, festooned with moss and lichen and ferns. Lower still lies a tangle of vine maple and other shrubs. Covering the ground is a luxuriance of ferns and a deep carpet of moss. Nurselogs, fallen giants which do not decay completely for centuries, support lines of seedlings which over those centuries grow into colonnades of new giants.

Yet the uniqueness of the rain forest depends not on plants alone: the open glades, startling amid the "permanent green twilight," are maintained by elk, without whose browsing and grazing the jungle would be absolute.

Yellow violets
Mushrooms
Oxalis

Hoh rain forest in fall

TREES AND FLOWERS

Only in Olympic National Park occur all four major forest zones of Western Washington. Confined to the ocean side is the Sitka Spruce Zone, of which the rain forest is a subzone. The Western Hemlock Zone, second-lowest there and lowest elsewhere, is dominated by the same trees except in different proportions and with the spruce absent. Above lies the snow-country Pacific Silver Fir Zone, noble fir and Alaska cedar the main associates. Highest is the Mountain Hemlock Zone, subalpine fir the principal companion; here closed forest opens into parklands and flower fields, often as low as 4000 feet.

In her book, *The Olympic Rain Forest,* Ruth Kirk says of the peninsula's west slopes, "more gigantic trees of more different species grow together than anywhere else in the world." Included are the largest known specimens of western redcedar (near Kalaloch), Douglas-fir (Queets River), western hemlock (East Fork Quinault), except for one in Oregon, Sitka spruce (Queets), red alder (Hoh); there also are record specimens of Pacific silver fir and subalpine fir.

The most spectacular flower show of the Olympics, barely surpassed in fame by the rain forest, is staged by the evergreen rhododendron *(macrophyllum).* The bloom begins along Hood Canal and the Strait of Juan de Fuca in mid-May and during June climbs the foothills, concluding in early July at about 3500 feet. In those weeks visitors come from far away to drive or walk through miles and miles of dazzling pink blossoms.

Rhododendron in foggy forest of Mount Walker, above Hood Canal

Sword fern and vanilla leaf in North Fork Quinault valley

Marymere Falls, on nature trail at Lake Crescent visitor center

Overleaf: Field of avalanche lilies on High Divide. 7965-foot Mount Olympus in distance.

WILDLIFE

Visit a single park and see both whales and mountain goats? Yes, and a profusion and variety of other wild creatures unequalled in America.

In springtime gray whales spout plumes of spray mere yards from astounded beachwalkers. All year the harbor seal swims through breakers, and sometimes a sea lion. Deer and bear and elk make tracks in sand, as do, especially in early summer when smelt are spawning on the shore, river otter, mink, skunk, marten, weasel, and raccoon.

The largest land animal is the Roosevelt elk, bulls weighing up to a half ton. In summer the bands graze highland grass but in winter are down low, and easily viewed, browsing the rain forest.

The black bear of the mountain interior has no knowledge of guns and is generally aloofly nonchalant about man except where he has been perverted by careless hikers' garbage. Deer are everywhere, as are the predators which keep them from overcrowding their habitat. Olympic is believed to have the largest cougar population of the national parks, but a visitor should not expect to see any, or bobcats either. A hiker, though, may glimpse or hear coyotes, which have expanded in numbers to fill the ecological niche of the wolf, exterminated about 1930.

Particularly on paths leading toward Mount Angeles from the Hurricane Ridge road, the park offers the easiest chance anywhere for a close look at the symbol of the crags, the mountain goat. One hardly needs leave roads to see the best-loved meadowland animal, the Olympic marmot, squatting fatly on a boulder, whistling a warning to its family, then scuttling into a hole.

Roosevelt elk at Hoh River campground

Deer on Hurricane Ridge

Marmot

Mountain goat nursing kid on Mount Angeles

Grouse

7365-foot Mount Anderson and cloud covered Enchanted Valley.

Herd of Roosevelt elk above Hoh Lake on the High Divide

Mountain goat above Glacier Meadow camp on the route to Mount Olympus

CLIMBING

Most Olympic rock is weakly-metamorphosed, closely-folded sediments eroded into rubble heaps easily walked up or scrambled. In The Needles, Sawtooths, and Mount Constance area the pillow lava extruded in submarine eruptions (one of the thickest lava formations in the world) is dissected into challenging and solid basalt crags. However, except for these the most popular climbs are either done as late-spring or early-summer snow ascents, such as the 6866-foot Brothers and 7743-foot Constance, or are glacier routes, such as 7365-foot Mount Anderson and, of course, Olympus.

The Olympics are remarkably icy for their modest elevation, having the lowest snowline in the old 48 states and 60-odd glaciers covering some 25 square miles. The obvious reasons are the cloudy-cool summers and the deluge of winter whiteness. Olympus receives possibly more than 100 feet of snowfall a year; a single storm once dumped 14 feet on the Blue Glacier. Some have speculated that were the peak a bit higher its frozen rivers might discharge bergs into the ocean, as they did 12,000 years ago during the Pleistocene Epoch; as it is, the Hoh Glacier descends to 3500 feet.

Much of the finest Olympic mountaineering does not seek summits. In summer, the all-day traverse from the Hoh trail-end to Queets Basin, over the Blue, Hoh, and Humes Glaciers, crossing Glacier Pass and Blizzard Pass, gives a sense of being somewhere in the Yukon. In winter, cross-country skiers and snowshoers on multiday treks experience strenuous Far North-like joys on close-to-home "poor-folk expeditions."

Climbers passing the Blue Glacier icefall on Mount Olympus

On the trail from Hoh River to Mount Olympus, looking up Glacier Creek to the White Glacier

HIKING

With nearly 600 miles of trails, connecting to more in the national forest, Olympic is supremely a hikers' park, offering short walks and long, easy and strenuous, at elevations from sealevel to glacier level, for every season, and for novice and skilled wilderness navigator alike.

Various roads and paths lead to the ocean beach, itself a 50-mile "trail" along the surf-swept boundary of the park.

All around the range are trails suitable for day trips and weekends sampling forests, alpine lakes, and broad-view summits.

There are splendid valley journeys: 18 miles up the Hoh River to the Blue Glacier; 28 miles up the Elwha to 3662-foot Low Divide and 19 miles down the North Fork Quinault — the way of the 1889-90 Press Expedition; 11 miles up the West Fork Dosewallips to 4464-foot Anderson Pass (here a sidetrail climbs to the Anderson Glacier) and 16-1/2 miles down the East Fork Quinault, descending the Enchanted Valley where snowmelt streams tumbling over cliffs in early summer give the other name, Valley of a Thousand Waterfalls.

There are superb ridge-running routes: the Grand Ridge trail, highest in the range, running the 6500-foot tundra crest 8 miles from Deer Park to Obstruction Point; the Skyline Trail, 20 miles through parklands above the North Fork Quinault.

And for the experienced wilderness backpacker there are innumerable magnificent off-trail ventures, the legend among them being the 20-mile traverse of the Bailey Range; to keep out pikers, the shortest trail approach to the start of the traverse is 14 miles.

Meadow trails are mainly snowfree from mid-July through September; while obtaining the required camping permit a hiker may gain current information from rangers. Back-country travelers must be sure to carry wool clothing and rain gear; Olympic weather is notoriously unpredictable, except for the certainty of being cold and wet most of the summer, presenting a constant threat of hypothermia.

Several guidebooks describing park trails, and other informative books and maps as well, may be purchased at visitor centers and local bookstores and mountain shops.

Overleaf: Early summer at Hoh Lake. Across the Hoh valley, Mount Olympus and Mount Tom

Rain drops on lupine leaves

OCEAN

Olympic National Park touches two quite different oceans. The "easy ocean," paralleled by Highway 101 from Ruby Beach to Kalaloch, is accessible by a number of short paths. Still, one can walk the dozen miles of beach southward from the Hoh River and only occasionally be aware of the road and never be bothered, as on so much of the Washington coast, by gasoline machines racketing along the sands.

The wilderness ocean, the last lengthy stretch of wild seashore between Canada and Mexico, may be approached by roads to Rialto Beach and the Hoh mouth, two 1-mile trails from near LaPush, and two 3-mile trails from Ozette Lake. The classic backpacks are the South Wilderness Beach, 16 miles from near LaPush to the Hoh, and the North Wilderness Beach, 20 miles from Rialto to Cape Alava. Each requires 3 days and tide charts to plan the daily schedule.

What does the wilderness ocean offer? Beaches of sand, beaches of cobbles, between steady-pounding surf and densely-jungled bluffs sliced by tangled creek gorges. Cliffy headlands, caves, arches, and sea stacks. Animals on land and water, birds flying and swimming. Indian pictographs and kitchen middens. Driftwood. Relics of wrecked ships.

It also offers the only pristine tidal-pool gardens on the Northwest coast, all those with auto access having been stripped bare by thoughtless collectors. Remember: *never disturb any living creature or plant. Leave it where you see it.* Enjoy the 15 varieties of seaweed — algaes that range from crusts on rocks to great grassy masses, in color are red, pink, purple, black, brown, olive, and green. Observe barnacles and mussels and limpets and rock oysters, snails and periwinkles and worms and chitons and sand dollars, anemones and sea urchins and hermit crabs and shore crabs and starfish — a community so rich in life that a single square yard of tidal pool may contain 200,000 animal organisms. Enjoy it all — and leave it all there for others to enjoy.

Anemones and starfish

Bald eagles

Driftwood

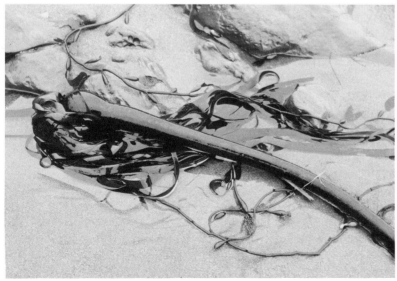

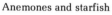

Kelp

The *General M. C. Meigs* at Portage Head, between Shi Shi Beach and Mukkaw Bay

Seagulls and the wilderness beach

Salmon leaping cascades of the Soleduck River, on way to spawning grounds in
fall

Three-ton anchor from the bark *Austria*, wrecked at Cape Alava in an 1887 gale

Toleak Point.

Sea stack at Rialto Beach

Winter storm at Ruby Beach

THE
MOUNT RAINIER NATIONAL PARK

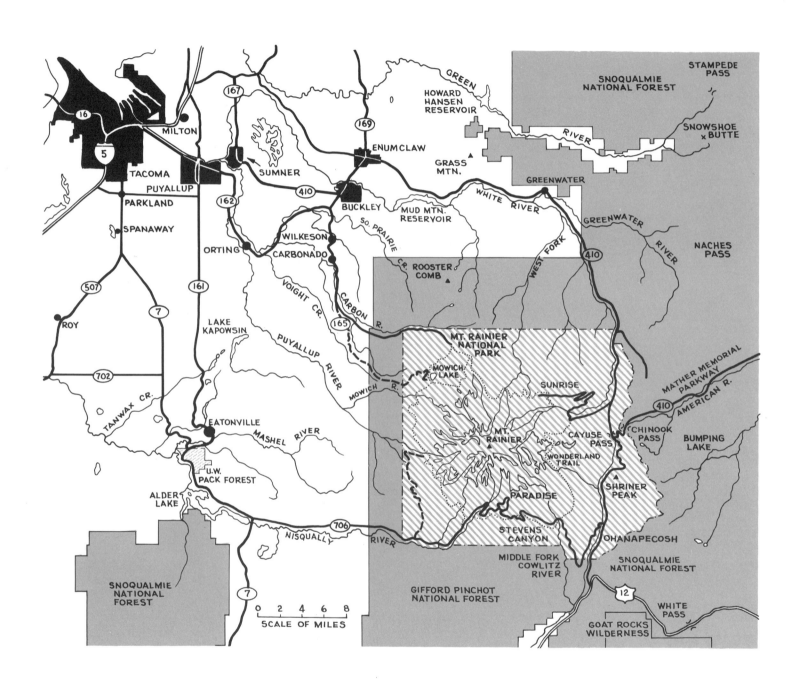

Previous page: Paradise flower fields

MOUNT RAINIER

Said John Muir after his 1888 climb to the crater, "Of all the fire mountains which, like beacons, once blazed along the Pacific crest, Mount Rainier is the noblest."

The stupendous white volcano, rising in just 45 miles from tidewater to 14,410 feet, standing 12,500 feet above valleys at its base, has no rival in the lower 48 states for tallness, for hugeness, for splendid isolation. Visible from far out in the semi-desert of the Columbia Plateau, miles offshore in the Pacific Ocean, atop summits in British Columbia and halfway down through Oregon, Rainier lords it over the Northwest.

Superlatives pile on superlatives. Winter storms dump snow by the skyload; in 1971-72 Paradise Valley recorded the greatest one-year snowfall ever measured at any official weather station in the world — 93-1/2 feet! Even in an average year the total is 50 feet, and a consequence is another pair of superlatives: the largest single-peak glacier system in the lower 48, yet so easily approachable that more Americans have walked to the edge of ice rivers here than in all other mountains of the nation combined.

But there is one last and stunningly contrasting superlative: Rainier displays the climax flower fields of the Cascade Range, the colors the more brilliant for the austerity above.

Indians knew well the peak they called "Tahoma" or "Takhoma," meaning "the mountain," with overtones of "highest mountain" or "snowiest peak." For centuries they visited the parklands in late summer, women to pick huckleberries, dig roots, collect herbs, and gather beargrass for basket-weaving, men to hunt deer, elk, goat, marmot, and grouse.

The earliest known written reference to the peak was made in 1792 by Captain George Vancouver of the British Navy, who while exploring Puget Sound noted in his log the "very remarkable, high, round mountain, covered with snow" and named it for his friend, Rear Admiral Peter Rainier. In 1833 Dr. William Fraser Tolmie, stationed at a Hudson's Bay Company trading post near modern Steilacoom, was the first white to reach the slopes, in the course of a "botanizing excursion." In 1852 a party of whites climbed to the top — which, however, very likely had been gained many times by Indians seeking diversion when hunting was slow.

Word of its wonders having been spread across the country by Muir and others, in 1899, preceded only by Yellowstone geysers and Sierra canyons and sequoias, the volcano was honored by creation of Mount Rainier National Park. Sorry to say, the vision of the pioneers fell short of the opportunity; they failed to establish a park big enough to constitute a complete and self-sustaining ecological and scenic entity. Citizen groups are pressing proposals to finish the job by enlarging the park to proper boundaries and supplementing it with wilderness areas in adjacent Snoqualmie and Gifford Pinchot National Forests, where logging has encroached on valleys and ridges that by natural right "belong" to The Mountain.

Though much of the park is protected wilderness, there is road access to Paradise Valley and Yakima Park and their panoramas of flowers and glaciers, and to Chinook Pass on the Cascade Crest, offering an arm's-length perspective. However, the steadily increasing number of visitors is expected ultimately to force partial replacement of private automobiles by shuttle buses, in order that people will not be crowded out of the park by their cars; even at present, problems of traffic and parking can be avoided by traveling to Paradise on the buses that run from Seattle and Tacoma, operated late June to early September by the Rainier National Park Company.

A quarter-million visitors a year leave gasoline fumes and racket behind on park paths. The 90-mile Wonderland Trail, encircling The Mountain and sampling deep-forested valleys and gaudy-blossomed ridges and stark moraines, is an American classic. So, too, is the Pacific Crest National Scenic Trail traversing the eastern boundary of the park. The most popular hiking centers are Paradise Valley and Yakima Park, with innumerable paths to delightful gardens and spectacular views. Most high-country trails ordinarily are free enough for walking from mid-July to October. Camping permits, issued at park entrances, are required for overnight hikes. All trails are described in *50 Hikes in Mount Rainier National Park*, available, with other useful books and pamphlets and maps, at visitor centers.

Overleaf: Moonrise over Mount Rainier and the Puyallup River

Overleaf: Yakima Park road winding through alpine flowers

VISITOR FACILITIES

The historic gateway to Rainier is the Nisqually Entrance, the only year-around automobile access to the high country. The road passes Sunshine Point Campground (always open except in occasional heavy snows), Longmire Inn (food and lodging May to October), and ascends by Cougar Rock Campground (June-October) to Paradise Valley. The all-year Paradise Visitor Center offers a cafeteria, museum displays, lectures, and naturalist-led walks. The central attraction for the nostalgic is Paradise Inn, providing meals and lodging mid-June to Labor Day. Constructed in the 1920s, the Inn poignantly recalls an earlier era of the park, and of America. Never again, surely, will there be such building materials as those used for the great beams and posts and table tops — centuries-old Alaska cedars salvaged from the clearing of the road right-of-way.

The White River Entrance leads to White River Campground (June-October) and Yakima Park, with snack and fountain service in summer, as well as a museum and ranger-naturalist walks.

The Stevens Canyon Entrance, near Ohanapecosh Campground (May-October), is an alternative approach to Paradise. The Carbon River and Mowich Lake Entrances are primarily for visitors prepared to hike some distance to attain views.

Many campgrounds are located in adjacent national forests. Food and lodging are supplied by numerous nearby resorts and communities.

Paradise Inn lobby

Paradise Visitor Center

Climbers approaching the summit crater, of which the highest rim is 14,410-foot Columbia Crest; beyond rises 14,112-foot Liberty Cap.

THE VOLCANO

A half-million years ago or so Rainier was born. Sometimes by exuding liquid rock, sometimes by exploding ash clouds skyward, The Mountain grew into a towering heap of alternating layers of hard, andesitic lava and softer ash and breccia. About 10,000 years ago it achieved maximum size, perhaps 1000-2000 feet higher than today; 14,150-foot Point Success and 14,112-foot Liberty Cap are remnants of the old cone. Then the summit collapsed inward, the catastrophe accompanied by explosion-triggered landslides. Eruptions resumed, building two new cones in succession, the last completed 2000 years ago, its rim being 14,410-foot Columbia Crest.

Does The Mountain still live? Indian legends of a "lake of fire" on top may recall eyewitness accounts by daring young men. The volcano long having averaged a major blast every 1000-2000 years, another — tomorrow — would be no surprise. Bursts of pumice are more frequent, the most recent confirmed blow-off occurring between 1820 and 1854. As climbers know

from steam caves melted in crater snows, there's a lot of heat down below.

Rainier is given to unpredictable fits of violence, most commonly sudden outburst floods and mudflows, some probably caused by blasts of steam concealed by the ice they melt. The largest of 55 identified mudflows, the Osceola Mudflow of 5800 years ago, perhaps resulted from the aforementioned destruction of the old cone; rumbling 45 miles down the White River, it covered lowlands beyond the mountain front in a sheet of debris 20 miles long and 3-10 miles wide. The Electron Mudflow of 500 years ago ran down the Puyallup River nearly to Puget Sound.

Ancient history? The Kautz Mudflow of October 1947 buried the Paradise road under 20 feet of boulders and gravel. In August 1967 an outburst flood from the South Tahoma Glacier inundated what was, until then, a campground, fortunately unoccupied — due to a closure for fire danger!

Rangers and scientists are keeping close watch on The Mountain, which is not dead, merely sleeping, and often uneasily.

Overleaf: Comet Falls, 320 feet high, on the trail to Van Trump Park

Overleaf: Reflection Lake and Mount Rainier from Stevens Canyon road

Devil's club

Trillium

Twinflower

Vanilla leaf

Indian pipe

FORESTS

Three of the four major forest zones of Western Washington are represented on Rainier, including 27 species of trees and hundreds of shrubs and herbs, ferns and mosses, lichens and fungi.

Low valleys of the park lie in the Western Hemlock Zone, whose other dominant trees are Douglas fir and western redcedar. The Nisqually Entrance, Carbon River, and Ohanapecosh Campground offer superb examples, the climax being the awesome Grove of the Patriarchs, with firs and cedars 250-300 feet tall, 8-10 feet in diameter, and 500-1000 years old. Far beneath sky-thrusting crowns the jungle of understory trees and shrubs billows from a green floor of ferns and mosses, brightened in April by flowers.

As the roads to Paradise and Yakima Park ascend valleys they enter the Pacific Silver Fir Zone, noble fir and Alaska cedar prominent among companion trees. This is distinctly snow country, melting out in May, the blossoming beginning soon after.

Highest is the Mountain Hemlock Zone, notable as well for subalpine fir and western white pine. Here the closed forest ends, opening into parklands where huddled clumps of trees stand amid fields white until July, then becoming a glory of summer color.

Above Paradise and Yakima Park trees grow steadily shorter and fewer, at last hugging the ground in wind-resisting mats, and less than a vertical mile from one of the world's most exuberantly lush accumulations of plant growth sprawl naught but arctic barrens and ice.

Facing page: Grove of the Patriarchs

Edith Creek near Paradise Inn

Eunice Lake and the northwest side of Rainier from Tolmie Peak

ALPINE FLOWERS

After long months of winter dormancy, alpine plants burst into sudden frantic life, hectic beauty, and nowhere more superbly than on high slopes of The Mountain.

The parks still are mostly frozen when lilies, anemones, and marsh marigolds, hurrying to be fruitful in the brief summer, push fresh whites and yellows from edges of snowfields and meltwater streams.

As snow dwindles to scattered patches, a meadow-roamer may well get drunk on the color and perfume of sun-warmed fields of blue lupine, red paintbrush, yellow arnica, and white aster, may go half-mad walking by — in a single hour — as many as 40 different flowers, each in its own proper nook where soils and moisture and temperatures fit individual needs.

Blossoms increasingly yield to seedpods, though brilliances linger in favored corners and new blooms appear, the blue gentian finally announcing that summer's end is near.

Yet the last of life can be the best. One may walk meadows red with dying huckleberry leaves, yellow with dying grass, white with the first powdering of the new winter, all glowing and glittering in low autumn sun, and descend from The Mountain in a mood of melancholy and joy, content.

Beargrass

Sitka valerian

Western anemone seedpod

Aster

Avalanche lily

Gentian

Avalanche lilies in Spray Park

Overleaf: Sunrise from 10,000-foot Camp Muir. In foreground, the Tatoosh Range. On the horizon (left to right), the Goat Rocks, Mount Adams, and Mount Hood, in Oregon

Cascade golden-mantled ground squirrel   Ptarmigan in winter plumage   Clarke's nutcracker

Raccoon   Bear

WILDLIFE

Of the 50 mammals on Rainier, the most abundant is man, a fact often of sorry consequence for other species. Deer and bear, for example, once were ubiquitous, but gave no pleasure to the discerning student of wild creatures. They are less frequently seen as people increasingly understand that offering handouts creates sickly beggar deer and dangerous "garbage junky" bears.

Only hikers are likely to observe bands of elk in meadows (and during the September mating season hear bulls bugling under the moon) and mountain goat on snowfields and crags. Coyotes occasionally let themselves be seen, cougar and bobcat virtually never.

The visible animal life is mainly small: chipmunks and squirrels dashing about picnic areas; the little pika squeaking from a rockslide, the louder when pursued by a weasel; the fat hoary marmot whistling from a boulder-top lookout, scampering into a hole on approach of anything that might conceivably be a coyote or bear.

No visitor fails to enjoy some or many of the park's 150 birds: water ouzels flying along creeks, the nutcracker and gray jay and junco robbing camps, grouse in parklands, ptarmigan in meadows, hummingbirds in flower fields, and high in the sky, ravens, hawks, and circling, circling golden eagles.

Facing page: Hoary marmot, Pinnacle Peak in distance

Cowlitz and Ingraham Glaciers and Little Tahoma

GLACIERS

The story of The Mountain for most of its recent life has been the dynamic tension between the piling up of lava and ash by eruptions and the tearing down by glaciers gouging cirques and digging troughs, carving cliffs and ridges and spires, and spilling the debris in moraines and rivers, whose muddy-milky color derives from rock flour that says, "ice mill at work."

Some flowing from the summit icecap, others from cirques at the 10,000-foot level, descending to 7000 or 5000 or even 3500 feet, Rainier's 15 principal glaciers and 25-odd lesser ones have a total area of 35 square miles — as much ice as in all the ranges of the lower 48 states outside the Cascades and Olympics, 6-1/2 times more than in Glacier National Park. The largest glacier in the lower 48 is the Emmons, 4 miles long and 1-3/4 miles wide.

Everywhere in the park and its hinterland are reminders of a formerly vaster dominion of winter. 15,000 years ago, in the Pleistocene Epoch, frozen rivers radiated down valleys to lowlands on every side; the Cowlitz Glacier was 65 miles long, reaching a point 33 miles beyond the modern town of Randle. For the past 5000 or so years glaciers have fluctuated, sometimes rather larger than now, sometimes rather smaller, though never melting completely. During the worldwide Little Ice Age of the 14th-19th centuries they attained their greatest post-Pleistocene extent, covering about 55 square miles in 1833, when Dr. Tolmie came botanizing. When the park was established the ice fronts were in a general retreat which continued until the 1950s; since then, however, they have stabilized or advanced, some as far as 1000 feet. The Mountain, indeed, gave the first hint of the trend toward a cooler, wetter climate subsequently noted everywhere on Earth.

Winthrop Glacier and Columbia Crest

Overleaf: Ice climbing on the Ingraham Glacier.

ICE CLIMBING

Taken a step at a time by an easy route, in calm summer weather by healthy, well-equipped climbers, Rainier is a simple ascent. Yet there are many, many steps and they come slow, very slow, in oxygen-lean air 2-1/2 miles up in the sky. Especially when ocean fogs seep into valleys, rise gradually to overwhelm all the world except companion volcanoes floating as snowy islands in a cloudsea, one may have the feeling of leaving Earth, entering a high wilderness as lonesome as the moon.

Nevertheless, by 1900 some 100 people (not counting an unknown number of Indians) had reached the crest and year by year the upward trickle swelled to a flood. Though as recently as 1955 only 200 climbers attained the crater, in 1971 the total was 2149 — and 1000-odd more tried and failed. On fine summer days long lines of pilgrims march in lockstep up the two popular routes — the one from Paradise used by the Rainier Guide Service, with an overnight high camp at 10,000-foot Camp Muir, then proceeding up the Cowlitz and Ingraham Glaciers; and the one from the White River, with high camp at 9500-foot Camp Schurman, then going up the Emmons and Winthrop Glaciers.

But these are just 2 of the 45 routes by which The Mountain has been climbed; on most it is rare for one party to see another, and this despite the fascination the icy mass holds. As granite walls of Yosemite are to the rock climber, so are glaciers of Rainier to the ice climber. If the Grand Teton is the nation's most famous big rock mountain, Rainier is its most famous big ice mountain. Further, Rainier is the "poor man's McKinley," in winter offering close-to-home challenges comparable to giants of the Alps, Alaska, and according to the Americans (all Rainier veterans) who stood atop Everest in May 1963, even the Himalaya.

Climbers (who before their ventures are asked to register with park rangers) cannot help but be enthralled by Dee Molenaar's book, *The Challenge of Rainier*, a history of ascents from the Indian era to the present. There they also will find described the High Orbit, a 4-day and 25-mile volcano-encircling expedition between the 7200-foot and 10,000-foot levels, crossing 20 glaciers, giving the cold wilderness feel of the Far North.

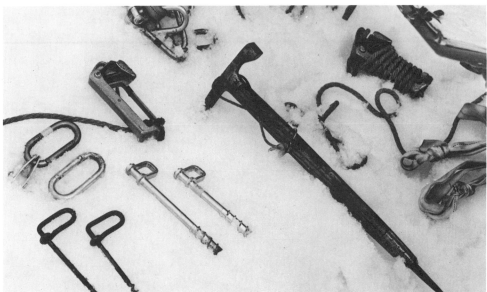

Ice-climbing equipment

Rappelling

Cutting steps

Crampons

Leaping a crevasse

Facing page: On the Winthrop Glacier

Paradise Ice Caves

Sunrise from Mazama Ridge

WINTER

The Rainier winter is long. Above 7500 feet, indeed, it is the sole season of the year and at meadow elevations normally lasts from late September to July. Yet despite the snow — or rather, because of the storms that unload such enormous amounts — downhill skiers prefer the better weather, safer slopes, and easier access of the Crystal Mountain Ski Area, adjoining the park in Rainier's rainshadow, and the nearby White Pass Ski Area.

The Mountain offers different winter pleasures. On high the expeditionary climber seeks his strenuous joy. Down low the forest trails, mostly bare all but several weeks, offer the philosopher room for solitary pondering, plus a chance to meet animals descended from chill heights and not expecting humans. In middle elevations the cross-country skier and the snowshoer find wilderness expanded far beyond summer bounds, temporarily reclaiming even roads — except those on which snowmobiles have not been banned, as ultimately they must be.

The Paradise road is the favorite starting point for tours on boards or webs into quiet forests and white-gleaming basins. Paradise itself is renowned as the Northwest's supreme family-play area. Demountable ski lifts, removed in summer so flowers and glaciers can be viewed without distraction, provide low-cost, elbow-free sport; weekends when commercial resorts are mobbed by thousands, several hundred people are a crowd here. A few stay on tow slopes, more go wandering, perhaps upward toward Panorama Point. Children ride inner tubes, throw snowballs, and build snowmen. And some folk, their romping years decades in the past, are satisfied to sit in the visitor center and look out to white-hung trees and up, up to The Mountain.

Paradise ski area

Paradise Inn and Tatoosh Range

Tatoosh Range from Paradise

THE
NORTH CASCADES NATIONAL PARK

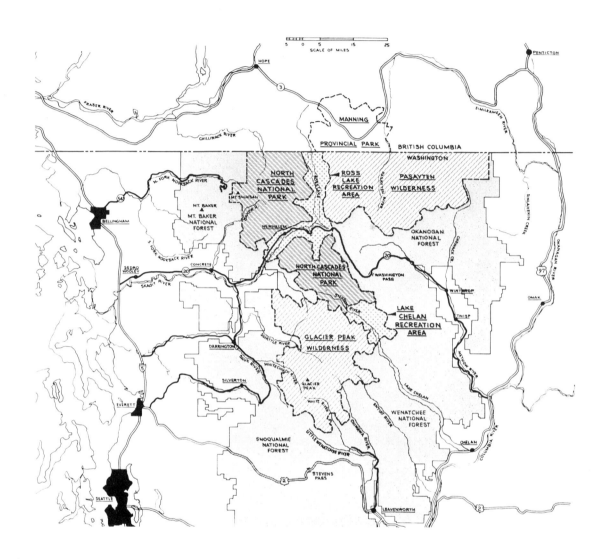

SCALE OF MILES

FRASER RIVER

CHILLIWACK RIVER

HOPE

MANNING

PROVINCIAL PARK

BRITISH COLUMBIA

WASHINGTON

SIMILKAMEEN RIVER

PENTICTON

M. FORK NOOKSACK RIVER

MT. BAKER

MT. SHUKSAN

NORTH CASCADES NATIONAL PARK

ROSS LAKE RECREATION AREA

PASAYTEN WILDERNESS

S. FORK NOOKSACK RIVER

MT. BAKER NATIONAL FOREST

NEWHALEM

OKANOGAN NATIONAL FOREST

SINLAHEKIN CREEK

OKANOGAN RIVER

BELLINGHAM

SEDRO WOOLLEY

CONCRETE

SKAGIT RIVER

WASHINGTON PASS

NORTH CASCADES NATIONAL PARK

WINTHROP

OMAK

97

STEHEKIN RIVER

LAKE CHELAN RECREATION AREA

METHOW RIVER

TWISP

DARRINGTON

SUIATTLE RIVER

BLUE RIVER

WHITECHUCK RIVER

GLACIER PEAK WILDERNESS

SILVERTON

GLACIER PEAK

WHITE RIVER

LAKE CHELAN

EVERETT

WENATCHEE NATIONAL FOREST

SNOQUALMIE NATIONAL FOREST

LITTLE WENATCHEE RIVER

COLUMBIA RIVER

ENTIAT RIVER

CHELAN

COLUMBIA RIVER

SEATTLE

STEVENS PASS

LEAVENWORTH

Previous page: *Mt. Challenger and Challenger Glacier from a snowmelt pool on the flank of Challenger Ridge*

74

THE NORTH CASCADES

Big Beaver Campground

For 500 miles from California through Oregon into Washington the Cascade Range is a long and narrow sea of green-forested lava ridges broken by a succession of high, island-like volcanoes. At Snoqualmie Pass the simplicity of design abruptly ends and in the final 150 miles to the Fraser River the underlying structures are a bewildering jumble of folded and faulted granitic and metamorphic and sedimentary rocks — plus two more volcanoes. This is the geologic province called the North Cascades.

Here the range attains its greatest width — 120 miles from Puget Sound lowlands to the Okanogan valley — and its greatest overall altitude, a half-dozen summits standing over 9000 feet and scores over 8000. But elevation alone merely makes plateaus; to create mountains dissection is required, and for them to be alpine the finishing work must be done by ice. The North Cascades abundantly qualify, boldly sculptured during the Pleistocene Epoch into sharp crags and deep valleys and still holding half the living ice in the old 48 states.

The maritime climate that piles up the snows that feed the glaciers, and the creeks and waterfalls and rivers, and lakes and ponds and marshes, also nourishes luxuriant forests and brilliant flower fields. The annual precipitation in meadows of Mt. Baker is 111 inches, and so much comes in winter the yearly snowfall averages 46 feet. To be sure, there is another side of the mountains, the sunny side, and as ocean winds empty out in the eastward flow precipitation dwindles to 34 inches at the head of Lake Chelan and a meager 12 inches in Pasayten tundras.

Though man entered the North Cascades thousands of years ago, the recorded history goes back only to 1811, when Alexander Ross, seeking a cross-mountain route for the fur trade, was the first white to follow Indians into the heart of today's wilderness. For nearly a half a century his venture was one of a kind, until English and American surveyors traversed the 49th parallel in 1857-61 to mark the international boundary. About the same time the army arrived, chasing Indians, and soon thereafter the prospectors in search of shining gold. Their numbers waxed and waned as they rushed here, rushed there, enthusiasm climaxing in the summer of 1897, when more people lived in the North Cascades than ever before or since; next spring most rushed off to the Klondike.

Recreationists and scientists began to travel the miner-built trails as "America's Alps" were publicized by railroads striving to boost tourist revenues. Exploiters came, too. In 1892 the townsfolk of Chelan, shocked at the slaughter of mountain goat and grizzly bear by Eastern and European sportsmen, raised the first call for a national park. Nothing came of it, nor of the other such proposals made at intervals of a decade or so over the next three-quarters of a century.

However, national forests were established covering most of the region and from the late 1920s to early 1940s the U.S. Forest Service recognized the scenic grandeur by designating portions as the North Cascades Primitive Area, the Mt. Baker Recreation Area, and the Glacier Peak, Monte Cristo, and Alpine Lakes Limited Areas. Unfortunately, after World War II Forest Service enthusiasm for esthetics faded, and though under public pressure it set aside the Glacier Peak Wilderness in 1960, citizen groups were so disappointed by the small size they revived the national park idea. Partial success rewarded their campaign in 1968, Congress creating the North Cascades National Park, the associated Ross Lake and Lake Chelan National Recreation Areas, and from a part of the old primitive area, the Pasayten Wilderness.

The legislation of 1968 encompassed a few scenic climaxes; the fate of the rest, however, remains to be settled. The Forest Service plans bits of additional wilderness and a variety of back-country, roadless, and scenic areas. Citizen groups applaud the plans as far as they go, but to preserve genuinely viable ecosystems are proposing a much more substantial expansion of wilderness, as well as of the national park and national recreation areas. Their companions across the border similarly are seeking new parks to protect the Canadian share of the range.

The years immediately ahead will be decisive, determining how much primitive beauty of the North Cascades will be saved for the lasting wealth of two nations, and of all mankind.

South from Slate Park, highest point accessible to automobiles in the State of Washington and offering a magnificent view of the Pasayten Wilderness

Skymo Falls on Ross Lake

Mt. Baker and the Baker River valley from Anderson Butte

PROVINCES

Though geologists consider the North Cascades a single province of Earth, politicians and bureaucrats have divided and subdivided the region into many a jurisdiction under a variety of different philosophies of management.

The British Columbia share of the range presently is dominated by logging, with the exception of Cathedral, Sapper, and E.C. Manning Provincial Parks, the latter crossed by the Trans-Canada Highway, the other two accessible from sideroads.

The bulk of the Washington mountains are in four National Forests, Mt. Baker, Okanogan, Wenatchee, and Snoqualmie, mainly devoted to logging wherever the trees have commercial value; however, some portions are likely to be placed in backcountry, roadless, or scenic areas and several already have special status.

Glacier Peak Wilderness, 458,500 acres, extends from the 10,541-foot volcano to Lake Chelan. Only horsemen and hikers can know the interior, but roads to the periphery up such valleys as the Suiattle permit easy samplings of lush forests and tumbling streams.

Pasayten Wilderness, 520,000 acres, sprawls from near Ross Lake east 45 miles to Okanogan country. Again, the inner solitude is purely for the long-distance roamer, but the Slate Peak road above Harts Pass tops a boundary ridge from which one can survey miles of lonesome peaks and valleys.

Mt. Baker is within a recreation area that also contains Heather Meadows, famous for the magnificence of 9127-foot Mt. Shuksan and the loveliest North Cascades gardens approachable by paved highway. Short walks add more flowers and views of 10,778-foot Baker as well.

In 1968 certain national forest lands were transferred to the National Park Service.

North Cascades National Park, 504,500 acres, is split in two pieces. No road touches the north unit, centered on the remote, spectacular Pickets and also holding most of Shuksan, but motorists can look to the interior from Heather Meadows and Harts Pass. The south unit, centered on the great peaks and glaciers reaching from 8868-foot Eldorado to 9200-foot Goode, is intruded by the very rough and narrow Cascade River and Stehekin River roads, both with fine views and splendid starts for hiking and climbing. Virtually the entirety of the present park is planned for inclusion in the National Wilderness Preservation System — not due to any Park Service prejudice against cars but because virtually every practical road route was deliberately omitted from the park when it was created.

Ross Lake National Recreation Area, 105,000 acres, is partly traversed by the North Cascades Highway, from which a tramway may someday be built up 7408-foot Ruby Mountain for panoramas of park wilderness. Seattle City Light dams have flooded (or dried up) most of this stretch of the Skagit River, which when free-running was the noblest stream in the range. A trail from Diablo Lake quickly enters venerable forests of Thunder Creek. A boat ride on Ross Lake followed by a walk up the Big Beaver valley leads to bird-teeming marshes and to groves of huge and ancient western redcedar, the finest left in the United States.

Lake Chelan National Recreation Area, 62,000 acres, includes upper Lake Chelan and the lower Stehekin valley. In summer a daily passenger boat departs in morning from Chelan, amid sagebrush hills, voyages 55 miles up the drowned channel of a Pleistocene glacier to cliffs rising dramatically to 8000-foot peaks, arrives at Stehekin in time for lunch, and returns downlake in afternoon. Visitors may complete the round-trip in a day or stop overnight or longer at lodges or campgrounds. A minibus shuttles passengers up and down the Stehekin road for camping, fishing, hiking, and climbing.

The Lady of the Lake *arriving at Stehekin. Above, Mt. McGregor*

Glacier Peak from flower fields on Meadow Mountain, above the White Chuck River

Aspen in autumn colors, along the Iron Gate road, eastern approach to the Pasayten Wilderness

The old mining and ranching town of Winthrop, at the east end of the North Cascades Highway, rebuilt to resemble its look of the 1890s

Liberty Bell Mountain from Washington Pass

Paul Bunyan's Stump and Pyramid Peak from the North Cascades Highway

NORTH CASCADES HIGHWAY

Opening of the North Cascades Highway in 1972 thrust an avenue of high-speed civilization through a section of the range that until then was one of America's largest remnants of pre-frontier wildland, for 90 air-miles from Stevens Pass north to Allison Pass completely free of machines.

Recognizing that the corridor must not be allowed to deteriorate into another Snoqualmie Pass, the National Park Service, U.S. Forest Service, and the State of Washington have agreed to exclude major developments from the central section. On the west, therefore, the last tourist facilities are at Marblemount and the last campground at Diablo Lake; on the east, Winthrop offers the last tourist services and Early Winters Creek the last campgrounds.

State Highway 20, as it is numbered on maps, extends 170 miles from Interstate 5 near Puget Sound to US 97 on the Columbia River. In an average year the middle 40 miles are open from sometime in June to sometime in October; avalanches and snowstorms and floods may cause temporary closures through early July and after mid-September.

The drive starts on the west with 47 miles along the pastoral Skagit valley to Marblemount and an exciting view to glacier-gleaming cliffs of Eldorado Peak. The next 25 miles up the Skagit Gorge give glimpses of the Pickets, a confrontation with Pyramid and Colonial Peaks, and an overlook of Ross Lake. A few high summits can be seen briefly in the 23 wooded miles up Ruby and Granite Creeks to 4840-foot Rainy Pass, from where a 6-mile climb leads to 5480-foot Washington Pass and Liberty Bell Mountain, a glorious granite tower now brutally scarred by dynamite and asphalt. A 19-mile descent through forests of Early Winters Creek ends in grass and sagebrush of the Methow valley, down whose broad glacial trough the highway continues 12 miles to Winthrop and 41 final miles to the Columbia River.

Lady slipper, a member of the orchid family, beside the Suiattle River trail

The Thunder Creek trail, one of the finest forest walks in the North Cascades

Tiger lily

Indian paintbrush

Elephant's head

Puffballs

Canadian dogwood

FLOWERS

Except for a few weeks of winter there is always a flower show somewhere in the North Cascades. Hundreds of plants, each in their own and proper times and places, celebrate life with blossoms large or small, bold or subtle.

Crusty, needle-littered snowpatches still are melting from low valleys when skunk cabbage erupts in garish yellow stalks and hoods, soon followed by the classic white trillium and the dainty violet, the start of a spring-to-fall succession of forest colors.

In highlands the impatient glacier lily thrusts through edges of retreating snowfields to start the brief, spectacular, summer pageant. Shortly, shooting stars and mimulus bloom by creeks, stonecrop and spreading phlox on dry rocks and sand. Heather slopes become radiant fields of pink bells and white bells, and entire mountainsides wind-dancing ensembles of yellow-and-white daisies, blue lupen, and scarlet Indian paintbrush.

And when the gentian, last flower of summer, adds a mournful blue to the ridges of yellowing grass and ripe huckleberries, below in the forest the rains of autumn bring yet another "flowering" as mushrooms sprout on rotten logs, push up from fallen leaves.

FORESTS

Ask any North Cascades wanderer the trees closest to his heart and he'll be hard-pressed to choose from the scores of coniferous and decidous species in the seven or so distinct forest zones.

In rainy west-side valleys stand green cathedrals of Douglas fir, western hemlock, and western redcedar, individual trees as thick at the base as a dozen feet, as tall as 250 feet, as old as 1000 years, the cool gloom beneath sky-hiding crowns a riot of vine maple and devils club and salmonberry and ferns and moss and more, much more.

In sunny east-side valleys cinnamon-gaudy trunks of Ponder-osa pine rise straight and far from grassy slopes, and beside rivers flowing through sagebrush steppes the white bark of quaking aspen shines in dappled shadows of breeze-rippling leaves.

At varying elevations the closed forest opens into upper park-lands, where clumps of lacy-limbed mountain hemlock and spike-topped subalpine fir are scattered over meadows of heather, sedge, and blossoms. The supreme glory of the east is the Lyall larch, the evergreen-that-is-not, needles turning bright orange in fall, dropping off the bare black winter skeleton, and sprouting again in a miracle of ethereal springtime green.

Highest of all is the "elfin timber," dense mats of pines and firs and hemlocks that cannot stand erect against fierce storms but for survival must hug the ground — even as, on occasion, must you and I.

Big Beaver trail through the cedar forest

Highwood Lake in Heather Meadows, fall colors, and Mt. Shuksan

The Coleman Glacier on Mt. Baker, from Bastille Ridge

GLACIERS

Half the wild ice in the old 48 states lies between Snoqualmie Pass and the 49th parallel — 756 glaciers covering 103 square miles.

In the big league of Canada and Alaska this is, of course, just a light frost. But if polar grandeur is lacking in the North Cascades there is a special intimate quality to its ice, which nowhere obliterates vast areas in sterile whiteness, everywhere contrasts poignantly with neighboring meadows and forests. A person can be dazzled without feeling overwhelmed.

Motorists gain their best near views of glaciers at Heather Meadows, looking to Mt. Baker and Mt. Shuksan, and on logging roads above Baker Lake which are blinding bright from the glare of Baker.

Innumerable trails take hikers to margins of white crystal barrens where climbers often spend a full day, or several days at a time, becoming subtly estranged from the realm of green life.

Is the Ice Age over and done forever? Probably not. The maximum recent extent of North Cascades glaciers was 17,000 years ago, but they descended a considerable distance during the "Little Ice Age" of the 14th—19th centuries, and after generations of subsequent retreat, in the mid-1940s began a decade of thickening and lengthening and since 1955 have held their own — several continuing to advance.

Air view of Nooksack Tower and the north face of Mt. Shuksan

Crevasse on the Challenger Glacier

Sunset from Sahale Arm, above Cascade Pass and the fog-sea of the Cascade
River valley. To the left, Mt. Johannesburg

Jack Mountain rising above Ross Lake, from Desolation Peak

HIKING

Valley walks in forest shadows beside loud rivers. Highland wanders by flowers and waterfalls and tarns. Afternoon strolls a mile or two from the road. Ten-day backpacks deep into wilderness. These pedestrian tastes and just about any other can be satisfied in the North Cascades.

No one season is everywhere best. Low-valley trails on the west side melt free of snow during March or April and are delightful in spring rains and the occasional bursts of sun. High meadows usually remain largely snowcovered until mid-July or even August and after several weeks of alternating mists and blue skies are whitened by fall blizzards.

The east side, the rainshadow, is beloved as a refuge from gray, often being sunny-bright when windward slopes are gloomy-drenched. Winter snows pile less deep and thus both low country and high open for hiking sooner — in fact, tundras of the far northeast are mainly snowfree by late June, a month earlier than gardens closer to the ocean.

Forest Service wilderness permits, issued at ranger stations, are required for hikes in the Glacier Peak and Pasayten Wildernesses. Park Service camping permits, issued at ranger stations and park headquarters at Sedro Woolley, are needed in the park and the national recreation areas.

Any number of marvelous trails can be found by studying a map or watching for signs; guidebooks, though, help make the most of a short vacation. Two that between them describe hundreds of hikes, short and long, with text, maps, and photographs, are *101 Hikes in the North Cascades* and *Trips and Trails, 1: Family Camps, Short Hikes, and View Roads in the North Cascades and Olympics.*

The Big Beaver valley, which will be drowned if Seattle City Light is permitted to raise Ross Dam

From Sourdough Mountain down to Gorge Lake, a reservoir drowning a portion of the Skagit Gorge

Glacier Peak sunset from Image Lake

Eldorado Peak from the Klawatti Glacier

CLIMBING

Much North Cascades climbing is simple rock-scrambling or snow-plugging. But there are also tall granite walls, turbulent ice-falls, and intricate bastions of glacier and cliff — indeed, the range offers most of the truly alpine challenges in the old 48 states. Unlike the civilized Alps, though, this country especially belongs to the wilderness mountaineer, the grandest prizes demanding tenacity and humility to beat through jungles, ford torrents, haul packs thousands of steep feet up jackstraw and thicket, suspiciously navigate fog-mysterious ridges — and all before even beginning to employ ice and rock craft on the sought-for peak.

The sharp little summits of the Monte Cristo vicinity are excellent for afternoon sport. The ridge-walking typical of the Pasayten is interrupted by the massive bulk of Jack and the crumbling towers of Hozomeen.

The two volcanoes, Glacier Peak and Mt. Baker, provide ice routes varying from moderate to severe. The mile-high north face of Baker's neighbor, Mt. Shuksan, is an American classic.

Cascade Pass is famous for Eldorado, Forbidden, Johannesburg, and Formidable. Southward from the pass begins the Ptarmigan Traverse, a legendary high alpine tour; anchoring the far end is mighty Dome Peak.

Among other climaxes are Bonanza, at 9511 feet the highest nonvolcanic peak in the Cascades, Liberty Bell, compared to the Dolomites for the soundness and airiness of its walls, and the remote Redoubt and Slesse.

The Pickets, though, uniquely embody the essence of the North Cascades. Located at the "pole of remoteness" of the range, the cold spires of the Fury Group and the Terror Group are miserable to approach, rough to climb, and when the weather isn't bad it's terrible. Here, for sure, the sunshine climbers are separated from the wilderness mountaineers.

Forbidden Peak from the Klawatti Glacier

Climber rappelling down Magic Mountain. Beyond, Sahale Peak, Boston
Peak, Ripsaw Ridge, and Upper Horseshoe Basin, a headwater of the Stehekin
River

Climbers on a pinnacle above the Honeycomb Glacier. Beyond, winter-white
Glacier Peak

Air view of the McMillan Cirque wall of the Southern Pickets. In center, The Pyramid and Degenhardt Peak

Looking south into the Glacier Peak Wilderness from Eldorado Peak

Fireweed in alpine miniature, beside Price Lake on the north side of Mt. Shuksan

SAWTOOTH NATIONAL RECREATION AREA

"A natural fastness of the mountains, the ingress and egress by a deep gorge." So were Stanley Basin and Sawtooth Valley to peace-loving local Indians, who fled there amid headwaters of the Salmon River when bedeviled by fierce Blackfeet raiders. Secure from attack they lived easy and well on salmon crowding the streams and deer and elk and mountain sheep the hills.

In 1824 the same Alexander Ross who in 1811 had been the first white man to enter what is now the North Cascades National Park led a Hudson's Bay Company expedition up tributaries of the Snake River. He and his companions probably were the first whites to see the ice-chiseled granite crags of the Sawtooth Range.

The discovery of gold to the north of the area in 1860 soon was followed by strikes in foothills of the Sawtooths and, after completion of a toll road in 1864, by intensive exploration within the "natural fastness" itself. The Indian era ended abruptly during the Nez Perce and Bannock Wars of 1877-78, when the Sheepeaters, mountain-living relatives of the Shoshoni, also grew restless and were rounded up and moved to a reservation.

Though cattle and sheep were brought in to feed the mining camps, not until around 1890 did large-scale summer grazing of Sawtooth Valley commence. In another decade year-round ranching began and by 1930 practically the whole valley was homesteaded. But not many homesteaders stayed. Summers there are delightful—and short. Winters are bitter—and long. Of the annual precipitation, varying from 60 inches on west slopes of the Sawtooths to 15 on the east, some 85 percent falls as snow. Winter temperatures drop to −50°F and often in summer go below freezing. Frozen out and starved out, homesteaders sold out to big ranchers and for years Ketchum was the nation's major shipping point of sheep and lambs. The result is seen today in ranges so overgrazed they will be generations if not centuries recovering, and in wildlife so depleted by usurping of their food supply and by hunting that big game rarely is seen by the average visitor.

In the 1930s, as livestock ranching began its inevitable decline, the few year-round inhabitants increasingly took to supplementing income by dude-ranching, stimulated by the fact that opening of North America's first lavish ski resort at nearby Sun Valley brought fame to southern-Idaho scenery and some outsiders returned in summer to enjoy the attractions centering on 30-mile-long Sawtooth Valley.

On the west, rising to over 10,000 feet, is the Sawtooth Range, one of the nation's finest examples of block faulting and alpine glaciation. In the uplifted granite batholiths have been gouged deep, U-shaped valleys holding moraine-dammed lakes, notably Alturas and Stanley and Redfish, the latter now the site of the area's Visitor Center. The high country has been sculptured into matterhorn peaks, aretes, cols, and hundreds of cirques filled by alpine lakes.

On the east, also rugged and lake-dotted and rising even higher, are the White Cloud Peaks, built of colorful limestones and old volcanic rocks, and the Boulder Mountains. Close to the southeast are the Pioneer Mountains.

In 1937 the U.S. Forest Service, the principal land manager since the 1905 establishment of the Sawtooth Forest Reserve, accorded one portion of the mountains deserved recognition by setting aside the Sawtooth Primitive Area. Under terms of the 1964 Wilderness Act, in 1972 this preserve, slightly enlarged, was by Congressional action designated the 216,000-acre Sawtooth Wilderness.

However, by that time the needs for scenic protection were urgent over a much broader area. With the great tourist rush of the 1950s came a proliferation of unregulated ticky-tack development threaten-

Bench Lake trail

ing to destroy the Old West feeling. And with a deepening concern for the land came growing objections to the overgrazing by cows and sheep. Bringing to a head and focusing mounting worries for the future was announcement by a mining company of plans to dig a huge open-pit molybdenum mine in the heart of the White Cloud Peaks, considered by some the most spectacular of all Idaho's mountains.

Uniting to confront the crisis, the Governor, members of the Congressional delegation and the state Legislature, and masses of the citizenry joined to campaign for a Sawtooth National Park. Predictably, they were strenuously opposed by those who wished to carry on with the mining, logging, overgrazing, hunting down surviving wildlife, and razzing around trails on motorcycles. In 1972 Congress took action—a compromise.

A 754,000-acre Sawtooth National Recreation Area was established, including the new Sawtooth Wilderness, Sawtooth Valley and Stanley Basin, and the White Cloud Peaks and Boulder Mountains. The U.S. Forest Service, the assigned manager, undertook a program designed to maintain the Western ranching atmosphere, enhance the frontier flavor of Stanley, and restore mining towns, while providing as before water sports on valley lakes, car-camping, and wildland recreation in the high country. It also continued studies for possible designation as wilderness of the White Clouds and Boulders and Pioneers.

Yet the ultimate status was left in doubt by Congress, for it directed the National Park Service to study the national recreation area and the entire surrounding region for a national park, Idaho's first.

Now, Sawtooth National Recreation Area. In years to come, Sawtooth National Park? That decision awaits.

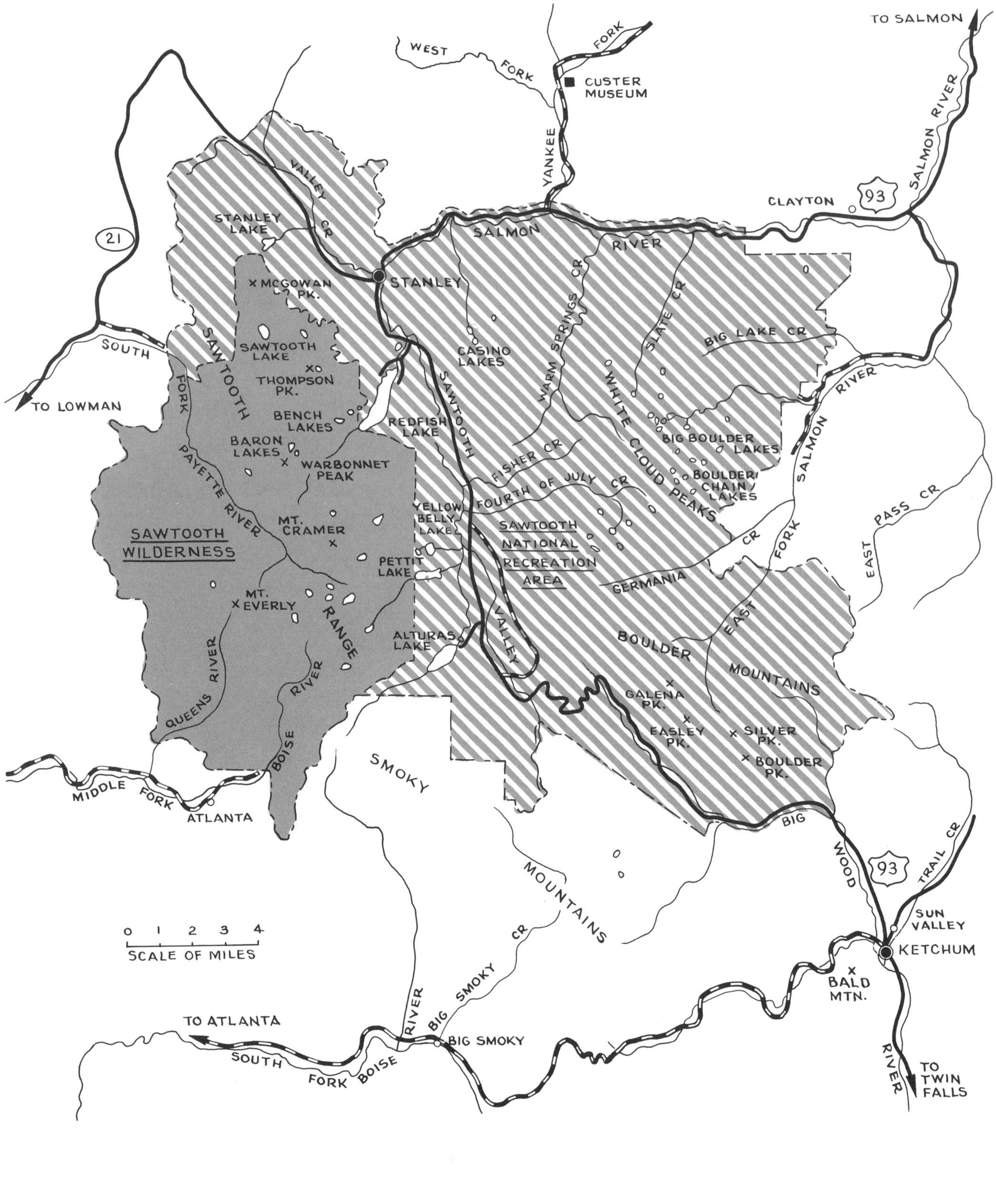
TO SALMON
WEST FORK
YANKEE FORK
CUSTER MUSEUM
CLAYTON
93
SALMON RIVER
STANLEY LAKE
VALLEY CR
21
SALMON RIVER
STANLEY
McGOWAN PK.
WARM SPRINGS CR
SLATE CR
BIG LAKE CR
SOUTH FORK
TO LOWMAN
SAWTOOTH
SAWTOOTH LAKE
THOMPSON PK.
CASINO LAKES
WHITE CLOUD PEAKS
BENCH LAKES
REDFISH LAKE
SAWTOOTH
BIG BOULDER LAKES
BARON LAKES
WARBONNET PEAK
FISHER CR
FOURTH OF JULY CR
BOULDER CHAIN LAKES
SALMON RIVER
EAST PASS CR
PAYETTE RIVER
YELLOW BELLY LAKE
MT. CRAMER
SAWTOOTH WILDERNESS
SAWTOOTH NATIONAL RECREATION AREA
PETTIT LAKE
GERMANIA CR
EAST FORK
MT. EVERLY
RANGE
ALTURAS LAKE
VALLEY
BOULDER
MOUNTAINS
QUEENS RIVER
BOISE RIVER
GALENA PK.
EASLEY PK.
SILVER PK.
BOULDER PK.
MIDDLE FORK
ATLANTA
SMOKY
MOUNTAINS
BIG WOOD
93
TRAIL CR
0 1 2 3 4
SCALE OF MILES
SUN VALLEY
KETCHUM
BIG SMOKY CR
BALD MTN.
TO ATLANTA
SOUTH FORK BOISE RIVER
BIG SMOKY
RIVER
TO TWIN FALLS

McGowan Peak

TRAILS

If lakes seem the major attraction of the Sawtooth Range, partly that is because scarcely any highland hike can be made without passing one or several or many, there being some 180 in the Wilderness alone. Generally melting free of winter ice and snow by mid-July, they are lovely in themselves, with shores of granite slabs and rockslides sprinkled with clumps of alpine trees and pockets of meadows, and provide splendid foregrounds for the serrate peaks, 42 of them over 10,000 feet.

Among popular introductory walks are the 4½-mile trail, gaining 1000 feet, to Bench Lake, and the 5-mile trail to Sawtooth Lake, another mile to McGowan Basin giving a degree of privacy. Though these and a handful of other lakes are mobbed, 170 others are not, and absolute solitude can be attained by traveling cross-country to the numerous cirques not entered by trails. Even in thronged areas the hiker can get away from it all by wandering up open, rocky slopes to the high ridges. Most peaks, indeed, have walking or scrambling routes to the summits. Still, there is fine sport for rock-climbers on the needles and sheer north faces.

Unlike the Sawtooths the White Clouds hide from roadside view behind foothills and thus the trails tend to have a thinner population. Emptier still are the Boulder and Pioneer Mountains. Doubtless the situation is temporary; certainly the peaks are in their own way as spectacular as the Sawtooths and the lakes and meadows as beautiful. The classic introduction to the White Clouds is the 8-mile hike beginning in sagebrush, climbing through forests, climaxing in the Little Boulder Lakes on the north slope of 11,820-foot Castle Peak, precisely at the site of the proposed open-pit molybdenum mine.

Sad to say, the hiker must choose his paths with care, nearly 200 miles in the national recreation area being officially open to trailbikes. Also frustrating is the fact that though even Stanley Basin was, in the old days, "a perfect hunter's elysium," only the high-country rambler has a fair chance of seeing elk, bighorn sheep, or mountain goat, much less a bear. Cows and domestic sheep, the latter grazing even in the Wilderness, have preempted most of the forage. Guns have decimated the wildlife and thoroughly spooked the survivors. In time, national park gunless and motorcycle-less status would restore the natural balance of the land and its native inhabitants.

Castle Peak from the Little Boulder Creek trail

Sawtooth Lake and Mt. Regan

Valerian

Monkshood

Shooting star

Red columbine

Blue huckleberry

Nuttall's linanthastrum

TREES AND FLOWERS

Receiving as little as 15 inches of annual precipitation, valleys of the Sawtooth country are sagebrush prairies that in places extend up foothills to elevations of some 6000 feet before reaching the lower timberline.

On west slopes of the Sawtooth Range is a Ponderosa Pine Zone. Elsewhere the lowest forests are in the Douglas Fir Zone, with much lodgepole pine and, along streams and lakes, quaking aspen. The high valleys and cirques lie in the Spruce-Fir Zone, dominated by Engelmann spruce, subalpine fir, and lodgepole pine. At the upper timberline is the Whitebark Pine-Barren Zone, gnarled and contorted pines growing from footholds in rocky ridges.

Among the 300 plant species are numerous flowering herbs and shrubs, the blossoming beginning on sagebrush prairies in early spring, progressing with the passing weeks upward through the open, park-like forests, concluding in late summer in sheltered nooks on peaks.

Yet the flower-loving visitor meets frequent disappointments. Though, surprisingly, highway shoulders occasionally may provide brilliant displays, over vast stretches cows and sheep have virtually destroyed the natural groundcover. Even in the Wilderness a hiker may enter what should be a glory of color to find the woolies have left naught but scraps. Only on high, in rock gardens beyond jaws of domestic beasts, can one be sure of a good show.

GHOST TOWNS

If the notion of a modern open-pit mine in the White Clouds horrifies, there is a ghostly fascination in evidences of the mining of olden days, the destructiveness limited by tools then available and nature having had many years to begin repairing the landscape.

Dating from boom times of the 1870s-80s are Vienna and Sawtooth City in Sawtooth Valley, Galena on the Big Wood River, Carristown near Fairfield, and many cabins moldering into the earth along roads and trails. The ghosts walk most vigorously in Custer, outside the national recreation area on the Yankee Fork of the Salmon River but being restored by the Forest Service to something like its appearance in 1888, when the population peaked at 3500. The General Custer Mine was started in 1876, the same year as the Last Stand of the 7th Cavalry, presumably the inspiration for the name. A museum displays relics. An interpretive trail leads by the mill that worked ore from seven large mines until 1904, recovering some $12 million in gold, and the blacksmith shop, carpenter shop, livery stable, general store, rooming house, dance hall, saloons, bawdy house, and jail.

Less fondly does a visitor view the gold dredge that from 1939 to 1942, and again from 1944 to 1952, extracted gold from the Yankee Fork. The dredge may still be seen, sitting where abandoned, and so may the 6 miles of devastated valley bottom.

Yankee Fork dredge

Old ranch house near Taylor Creek

Spatter Cones and Big Craters cinder cones

CRATERS OF THE MOON NATIONAL MONUMENT

Craters of the Moon! Surely not a fit place for man. Surely this convulsion of nature occurred just yesterday and violence might resume any moment. Is it truly safe to be here?

Probably. Though perhaps the newest fissure eruptions in the conterminous 48 states, the last of these wellings up of hot rock happened some 1600 years ago. And if those were hot times they were relatively quiet; Indians might have watched the show from a few hundred yards off and felt wonder but not terror. Certainly they retained no superstitious dread; camp artifacts are found amid the formations, which were used as shelter or even strongholds to baffle attacking enemies. White pioneers avoided the flows not from fear but an understandable reluctance to crawl over piles of slag. Only in the age of tourism did the area become widely known beyond Idaho settlers, at whose prideful urging Congress established in 1924 Craters of the Moon National Monument.

CRATERS OF THE MOON NATIONAL MONUMENT

The 83-square-mile preserve is located on the north edge of the Snake River Plains at the foot of the Pioneer Mountains. Southwest 18 miles from the town of Arco, Highway 20/26/93A cuts across the corner. A short spur road leads to the campground and the Visitor Center interpretive displays. A 7-mile loop drive samples the outdoor museum and gives access to the five nature trails, as short as the 20-minute walk in Devils Orchard, as long as the 2-hour hike to Great Owl Cavern. Centered along the Great Rift, a zone of crustal weakness through which lava rose from depths of 20-30 miles, 35 cones and vents and 30 flows have been identified.

The flows, all of basaltic lava, are of two kinds. Pahoehoe emerged very hot, about 2000°F, and very liquid. Quickly cooling on top and scumming over as motion continued, flows gained a smooth, billowy, or ropy surface with a variety of twists and folds, bumps and holes. Aa, cooler or less gassy and thus more viscous, flowed like slush ice, forming extremely rough masses of "clinkers."

Three types of cones are represented. Cinder cones, smooth-sided, symmetrical heaps of loose black cinders, were built by the fall-out of gas-filled lava froth tossed in the air by fire fountains. Denser than cinders are bombs, less-gassy lava blobs more or less streamlined during flight. Some of these cones are the product of many burpings over many centuries; an example is Big Cinder Butte, 6516 feet in elevation and rising 800 feet above the plain, one of the largest purely basaltic cinder cones in the world. Grassy Cone, on the other hand, derives from a single eruption that may have lasted merely several days.

The monument holds one of the world's most perfect chains of spatter cones, built by smaller fire fountains from which viscous clots of lava fell close to vents, forming steep-sided cones of small height and diameter.

Lava cones, really lava domes, very broad and rising inconspicuously to only 50 feet or so, resulted from quite peaceful oozings of liquid rock. In these are the lava-tube caves, chambers drained of still-running lava after the surface hardened. One of the most impressive, Great Owl Cavern, is 500 feet long, 40 feet high, and 50 feet wide.

Lunar-sterile the landscape indeed seems from a distance. *This* Moon, however, has a gentle side, supporting more than 200 species of plants. On north slopes, cooler and moister in summer than the arid, scorched plains, are sparse forests of limber pine. On open barrens grow sagebrush, bitterbrush, and rabbitbrush and in crevices such tough shrubs as white mockorange and tansybrush. But the gardens of spring are the miracle; one cannot help be startled and delighted seeing on bleak wastes of black cinders the brilliant yellow or pink blossoms of dwarf buckwheat.

A visitor need not stir far from the road to view most of the spectacular phenomena. Reserved for the experienced backpacker, though, is the supreme experience. More than half the monument is wilderness penetrated by few paths. Those adventurers who navigate by map and compass the 10 miles south to Vermilion Chasm feel they have, for sure, walked on the Moon.

Lava molded around a fire-charred log. The wood burned but the shape remained

OREGON CAVES NATIONAL MONUMENT

A quarter-century after Tom Sawyer and Becky Thatcher got lost in a Missouri cave, Elijah Davidson was hunting in the Siskiyou Mountains of southern Oregon and lost his dog. Following howls of canine pain into a hole in a hillside, he found the Oregon Cave and, when out of matches, lost himself. Soon, however, he stumbled into daylight, as did the dog, somewhat scratched and considerably mortified by a tangle with a bear.

From that day in 1874 the cave drew local adventurers, as well as a succession of pioneer entrepeneurs striving to establish a profitable tourist attraction. Their hopes were disappointed but they did lure such distinguished visitors as Joaquin Miller, "Poet of the Sierra," who in public print praised beauties of "The Marble Halls of Oregon," which in 1909 were proclaimed by President Taft the Oregon Caves National Monument.

Despite the plural name, there in fact is a single cave with an estimated 3 miles of known passageways. The largest of the some 25 rooms, the Ghost Room, is 40 feet high, 50 feet wide, and 300 feet long. Other features picturesquely named are Paradise Lost, Neptune's Grotto, Joaquin Miller's Chapel, Banana Grove, King's Palace, Dante's Inferno, and Wigwam. The tour led by concessioner guides covers 0.6 mile in about 1¼ hours.

The monument is tiny, a mere 480 acres, but surrounded as it is by a national forest utterly devoted to timber harvest, increasingly is treasured for preserving a sample of pristine mixed-conifer forest, a superb natural setting for the cave. Access is via Highway 199 connecting Highway 101 and Interstate 5; from Cave Junction, Highway 46 winds 20 miles to the cave entrance, located at an elevation of 4000 feet in the side of 6400-foot Mt. Elijah.

Though small compared to others in the nation, the Oregon Cave is the best-known in the Northwest and offers the region's only opportunity for the average person (that is, not a trained spelunker) to view the processes that form a limestone cave.

In the beginning millions of years ago was a sea inhabited by marine animals with shells of calcium carbonate. Deposited on the sea floor, these were compressed and hardened to limestone rock which during the mountain-building era was transformed by heat and pressure into marble in a belt 4 miles long and up to 400 feet thick.

Through fractures in the rock seeped rainwater charged with carbonic and other weak acids from decaying vegetation, dissolving the calcium carbonate and slowly hollowing out caverns, which at this stage were water-filled. Later, as outside streams cut valleys deeper or the land was uplifted, the caverns drained and became mostly air-filled.

Then commenced the shrinking of the caverns, the dissolved carbonate precipitating out from trickling water as it evaporated. Drips through air formed dripstone, icicle-like stalactites suspended from cavern roofs, stalagmites building up from the floors, the two when joined making columns. Flows down walls formed flowstone, layered, drapery-like deposits of travertine.

The Oregon Cave is an active or "living" cave. Unseen by the visitor, in lower portions of the formation new caverns, water-filled, continue to grow. During a tour one observes the sequel, the dripping and flowing that over the eons ultimately will plug the old caverns with solid rock.

Deer near parking lot

Steller's jay

OREGON CAVES NATIONAL MONUMENT

Joaquin Miller Chapel

JOHN DAY FOSSIL BEDS NATIONAL MONUMENT

The only thing John Day, a member of the 1812 fur-seeking expedition that founded Astoria, did for the river and surrounding country was to give them his name while struggling to get out of the area alive. Fifty years passed before white men arrived in force, initially in a gold rush to nearby Canyon Creek, then to graze cattle. In 1864 Thomas Condon, a minister and amateur geologist from The Dalles, discovered the fossil beds, which in succeeding decades were studied by such noted scientists as Joseph LeConte and John C. Merriam.

Later visitors were less thoughtful. Souvenir hunters ravaged the fossils, motorcyclists gouged the strikingly-beautiful red-and-green strata of the Painted Hills, and spray-can "artists" virtually obliterated the 2000-year-old Indian pictographs of Picture Gorge. Year by year became more urgent the need for better protection against vandals than could be provided by three existing Oregon state parks; therefore, in 1974, they and buffer lands were placed by Congress in a 14,402-acre John Day Fossil Beds National Monument.

The monument lies inside a rough square bounded by Interstate 80 along the Columbia River to the north, Highway 26 to the south, and Highways 97 to the west and 395 to the east. Administrative headquarters are 40 miles east in the town of John Day.

With annual precipitation of 12 inches, this section of east-central Oregon is semi-desert. The ridges, up to 3500 feet in elevation, are covered sparsely by sagebrush and rabbitbrush, a scattering of juniper, and patches of grass. In the canyons, sliced as deep as 1500 feet, willows and cottonwoods grow along tributaries of the John Day River, a part of Oregon's Scenic Waterways System. The monument has three separate parts: the Sheep Rock Unit, the largest and holding the most widely-known and diverse geologic and paleontologic resources and thus chosen as site of the Visitor Center; the Painted Hills Unit, famed for its wide variety of plant and animal fossils; and the Clarno Unit, displaying the oldest rock formations.

The monument is unique in the nation for portraying so vividly in so compact a space so lengthy a portion of Earth's history, covering six geologic epochs, four in the Tertiary Period and two in the Quaternary. More than 120 fossil mammals have been found, ranging in size from tiny mice to huge rhinoceroses and oreodonts, as well as fossil leaf imprints and petrified wood buried and preserved by volcanic ash.

In the Eocene Epoch of 37 million years ago the climate of the John Day Basin was subtropical. Volcanoes rose in the Cascades while eastern Oregon was invaded by a warm sea. Among palm, fig, avocado, pecan, and walnut trees roamed rhinoceroses, four-toed horses, tapirs, and crocodiles.

In the warm-temperate climate of the Oligocene Epoch (25 million years ago) the Cascade Range was eroded to low hills. Among dominant animals were oreodonts, tapirs, tiny camels, giant pigs, saber-tooth cats, and horses with three toes.

In the mild-humid Miocene (18 million years ago) lava flowed over much of Oregon. Gone were camels and tapirs but remaining were horses, pigs, and cats.

In the again warm-temperate Pliocene (6.4 million years ago) volcanic eruptions in the Cascades were accompanied by lava flows to the east. Rhinos and camels returned, joined by antelope, bear, mastodons, and horses with hooves.

Painted Hills

Indian pictographs in Painted Gorge

The Pleistocene (1 million years ago) brought large glaciers to the mountains and vast lakes to south-central Oregon. Vanished were bear, antelope, and rhino but joining horses, camels, and mastodons were giant beavers.

Finally came the Recent Epoch, with retreat of the glaciers, building of today's Cascade volcanoes, and, in John Day country, the erosion of overlying rock which exposed the fossil beds.

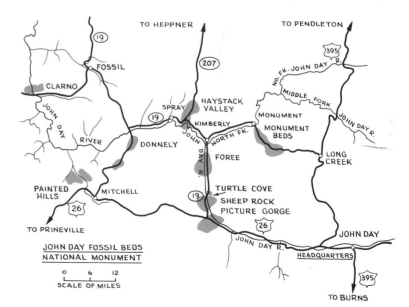

JOHN DAY FOSSIL BEDS
NATIONAL MONUMENT

0   6   12
SCALE OF MILES

Phantom Ship

Crater Lake and Wizard Island

CRATER LAKE NATIONAL PARK

KLAMATH BASIN NATIONAL WILDLIFE REFUGES
LAVA BEDS NATIONAL MONUMENT

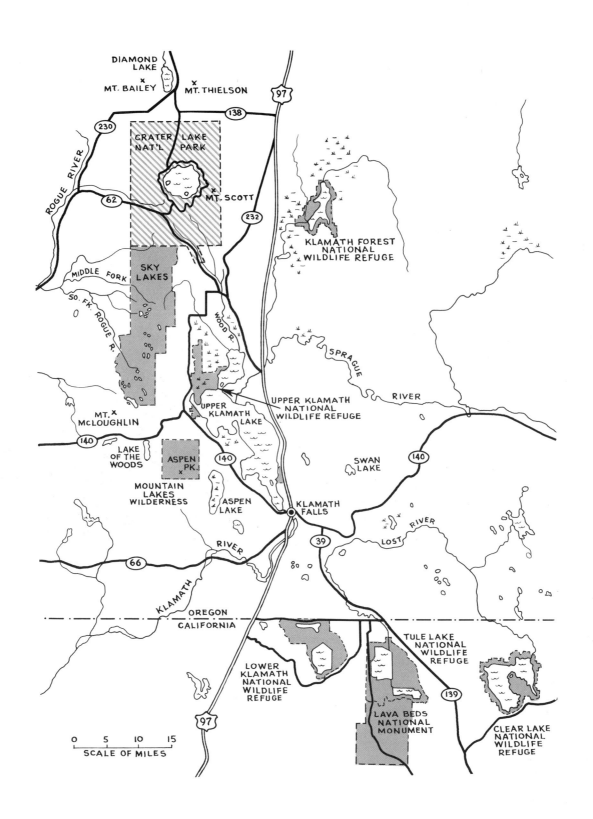

DIAMOND LAKE

× MT. BAILEY × MT. THIELSON

97

138

230

CRATER LAKE NAT'L PARK

ROGUE RIVER

62

× MT. SCOTT

232

MIDDLE FORK

SKY LAKES

KLAMATH FOREST NATIONAL WILDLIFE REFUGE

SO. FK. ROGUE R.

WOOD R.

SPRAGUE

RIVER

MT. × McLOUGHLIN

UPPER KLAMATH LAKE

UPPER KLAMATH NATIONAL WILDLIFE REFUGE

140

LAKE OF THE WOODS

ASPEN PK. ×

140

SWAN LAKE

140

MOUNTAIN LAKES WILDERNESS

ASPEN LAKE

KLAMATH FALLS

39

LOST RIVER

RIVER

66

KLAMATH

OREGON
CALIFORNIA

LOWER KLAMATH NATIONAL WILDLIFE REFUGE

TULE LAKE NATIONAL WILDLIFE REFUGE

97

LAVA BEDS NATIONAL MONUMENT

139

CLEAR LAKE NATIONAL WILDLIFE REFUGE

0   5   10   15
SCALE OF MILES

CRATER LAKE NATIONAL PARK

The Ouxkanee, People of the Marsh, dwelt between two great mountains. To the south rose the lofty white dome (nowadays called Mt. Shasta) that was the favorite resting place of Sahale Tyee, chief of the upper world. To the north stood the grim mass (nowadays remembered as Mt. Mazama) containing the passageway from which Llao, chief of the lower world, emerged now and then to glower over the countryside. The people often saw him there, a menacing darkness above the summit snows. The chiefs quarreled and Llao thundered forth burning rocks which fell upon the Ouxkanee. They thought the rain of fire was punishment for wickedness; to atone for community sins, the elders climbed the peak and lept into the flames. Touched by the sacrifice, Sahale took pity and drove Llao to his proper domain. The mountain fell in upon the lord of darkness and sealed his door and never again was he seen. The pit filled with serene waters and the Ouxkanee at last were free of constant fear.

The Ouxkanee (known since early 19th-century visits by Canadian trappers as the Klamath, from French words meaning "land of white fogs") shunned the silent spooky lake amid the ruins of Llao's mountain. White men did not learn of its existence until June 12, 1853, when John Wesley Hillman set out from the brandnew mining boomtown of Jacksonville in quest of the fabled Lost Cabin Mine, ascended a high point for a look around, and gazed down astonished into what he called Deep Blue Lake.

Over the next dozen years three parties applied other names — Blue Lake, Lake Majesty, Great Sunken Lake. Their wonderment was best expressed by a soldier who refused to believe it was a lake. Said he, "It ain't so! That's the *sky* we're looking at. How we got so far above it, I'll be danged if I know."

In 1869 a group of Jacksonville vacationers recognized the volcanic origin and gave the name that stuck, Crater Lake — though in fact the huge bowl, 5-6 miles in diameter, is not a *crater* resulting from lava outpourings but rather a *caldera* formed by the mountain's collapse into the emptied magma chamber.

The first photograph of the lake, taken in 1874 by Peter Britt of Jacksonville, spread its fame. However, 1885 brought the most significant visitor, William Gladstone Steel, a Portland mountain-climber who decided this "eighth wonder of the world" must have the protection only a national park could provide.

Responding to Steel's appeal, President Cleveland withdrew ten townships of the public domain from private preemption. In 1886 the U.S. Geological Survey conducted a detailed study and from the boat *Cleetwood* (built in Portland, hauled through forest wilderness by wagon and laboriously lowered down cliffs to the water) took soundings showing the lake to be fantastically deep. Subsequent measurements have put the bottom 1932 feet below the surface — the deepest lake in the United States, second-deepest in the Western Hemisphere, and seventh-deepest in the world.

Steel furthered his cause in 1896 by leading to the lake an outing of the Mazamas, a Portland mountaineering club, and with them formally giving the memory of Llao's largely vanished mountain a name, Mazama (Spanish for "mountain goat"). Days later he gained crucial support when there gathered on the caldera rim John Muir,

Diamond Lake and Mt. Thielsen

Gifford Pinchot, and companion members of the federal land commission traveling the West on an inspection tour that was to make conservation history. These distinguished and influential men came, saw, and were conquered. On May 22, 1902, President Theodore Roosevelt signed into existence the 250-square-mile Crater Lake National Park; only five of our parks are older.

In 1905 the first horseless carriage attained the rim. Though it was as much pushed and pulled as driven, each summer the track improved and the machine-swarm grew; by 1919 the lake was encircled by a rude road and had become a standard stop on sightseeing rambles around the West.

Now, as then, visitors are drawn by Earth's most spectacular caldera, gaudy colors of lava cliffs contrasting with the broad expanse of sky-pure, incredibly-blue water.

But the beauty is not all. For the sensitive there also are shudders, vicariously sharing the terror of the Ouxkanee during the destruction of Llao's mountain, a catastrophe that happened, as geologists measure time, a snap of the fingers ago.

Crater Lake and the lichen-colored Palisades

Phantom Ship and Crater Lake

Logs buried in pumice

Glacier-made scratches ("striations") near Merriam Point

GEOLOGY

For at least 40 million years the Crater Lake region intermittently has been a land of fire. Green ridges to the west are dissected remnants of ancient lava flows and volcanoes. Brown plains to the east were formed by enormous outpourings of fluid rock. Within the past 3 million years began still another era of violence, volcanoes large and small erupting the full length of the Cascade Range from California to British Columbia.

Perhaps few episodes in this chaotic history have matched the dreadful drama of 4600 B.C. Llao's mountain, or Mt. Mazama, then was a smaller neighbor of Sahale's mountain, or Shasta. Though not, as once thought, a perfect cone standing 12,000-14,000 feet above sealevel, but rather an asymmetric group of overlapping cones, the summit rose to about 10,000-12,000 feet, dominating the vicinity. On the south side glaciers flowed 3-4 miles from high cirques down over the sites of today's Rim Village and park headquarters; thousands of years earlier they had extended a dozen miles farther out the valleys.

This was the scene when Llao was seized by his last fury. With earth-shaking groans and bellows, tremendous explosions blasted clouds of ash into the stratosphere. Pumice piled 10 feet deep near the peak and was carried by winds at least 600 miles north and east, blanketing an area of 350,000 square miles.

Not all the lava shot skyward. Some welled over the crater rim and in *glowing avalanches* of superheated gas and incandescent magma and house-sized boulders roared at speeds in excess of 100 miles an hour to Diamond Lake and Klamath Marsh. The hot hurricane leveled forests and burned them to charcoal — which scientists have used, by carbon-14 dating, to establish the time of the cataclysm as approximately 6600 years ago.

When 12-15 cubic miles of Mt. Mazama had been strewn around eight states and two Canadian provinces, the shattered summit collapsed into the cavity previously occupied by magma. After lesser eruptions built cones on the caldera floor, notably the one now called Wizard Island, came the final and quiet act of the drama, the pit gradually filling with rainwater and snowmelt.

Everywhere in the park are reminders of the hot old days: charcoal logs and stumps of quick-burned forests; layers and dikes of lava; beds of pumice; erosion-dissected glowing avalanches, as at The Pinnacles, where hot gases escaping from the cooling mass fused the pumice, the vents becoming "fossil fumaroles" as softer surrounding ash was eroded away.

There is also evidence of the cold old days: Kerr Notch and Sun Notch in the caldera rim, and Munson Valley, the beheaded lower stretches of U-shaped glacier troughs; rock buttresses and slabs polished and scratched by moving ice.

Is Llao forevermore banned from the upper world? Maybe, and maybe not. Anyhow, Mt. Mazama surely deserves a rest.

FORESTS

Crater Lake country presents an exceptional variety of forests in relatively small compass. During a several-hour drive a visitor may experience seven or eight quite different vegetation zones.

Approaching the park from the west, the highway ascends three zones: the lowest, characterized by grassy savannas and oak groves; next, a tall-tree, cool-shadow assemblage of such conifers as Douglas fir, Ponderosa pine, incense cedar, and sugar pine; above that, a belt with many of the same species but dominated by white fir. Within the park the road climbs into the zone of lodgepole pine, accompanied by western white pine and Shasta red fir.

The approach from the east, starting in a semi-desert of lava and sagebrush dotted by shrubby western juniper, rises to the lovely realm of the Ponderosa pine, with water-loving quaking aspen along creeks. At any elevation, west or east, may be found extensive stands of lodgepole pine, a pioneer species that after 6600 years still has not completed its assigned role of reclaiming the pumice barrens.

From about 6200-6500 feet upward to the highest summits the park is occupied by the zone of mountain hemlock and associates, among them Shasta red fir and subalpine fir. As elevation is gained the continuous forest opens into a mosaic of meadows and tree clumps. Finally, stubbornly gripping rocky crests, are stunted and gnarled whitebark pines, wind-sculpted veterans of the storms.

Ponderosa pines near the park's southeast entrance

Overleaf: Golden-mantled ground squirrel

Vidae Falls

TRAILS

A dozen-odd short and easy paths lead in several minutes or a leisurely half-hour from Rim Drive through flower gardens and ice-scratched lava to views of Crater Lake grander than those beside the road.

Of the longer walks, a prime example is the 1.7-mile trail up 8060-foot Garfield Peak, providing a stunning lake overlook. Another is the 2.5-mile ascent of 8926-foot Mt. Scott, highest point in the park, giving a more distant perspective of the lake (and the supreme opportunity to *feel* the missing 15 cubic miles of old Mt. Mazama) plus a panorama over Klamath Valley marshes, western forests and eastern lava plains, and up and down the row of Cascade fire mountains from Mt. McLoughlin and Mt. Shasta south to Mt. Thielsen, Diamond Peak, and Three Sisters north.

The Pacific Crest National Scenic Trail crosses the west side of the park; southward it winds 25 miles through wooded ridges and plateaus of the Sky Lakes wilderness, sprinkled with innumerable small lakes and subalpine meadows.

North of the park are two fine viewpoints. The 8363-foot summit of Mt. Bailey requires a 3000-foot ascent — strenuous, but worth the sweat. A second popular trail climbs in 4 miles from Diamond Lake to wide-horizon rockfields under the final precipice of 9172-foot Mt. Thielsen, a glacier-stripped volcano core that is now, with Mt. Mazama merely a memory, the dominant peak of the area.

On the trails the visitor has the best opportunities to observe the park's abundant wildlife: a host of birds small and large, from hummingbirds to eagles; such little animals as chipmunks, squirrels, and pikas, such middle-sized ones as the mountain beaver, pine marten, red fox, and coyote, and such big ones as mule deer, black bear, and elk.

Discovery Point trail

False Solomon's seal

Heart-leaved arnica

Western pasqueflower

Spreading phlox

Steershead bleeding heart

FLOWERS

Gaining the 5000 feet from Crater Lake National Park's lowest elevations to its highest is the equivalent, so far as plant life is concerned, of journeying from the middle of the Temperate Zone nearly to the Arctic Circle. Each spring the flower display makes that journey, following upward the edge of the retreating snow. Middle or late May brings blossoms to valley forests. In the first week or two of June snowfree knolls amid the general whiteness of the caldera rim are splashed with color. By July early-bloomers are in full glory on the rim, joined as the weeks pass by more deliberate species, building to the exuberant climax usually in late July or early August. As summer moves toward fall, seedpods mingle with late bloomers until in frosty September the seeds drop or blow away in the wind and leaves turn red and yellow and plants prepare for the return of the snows and the longest season of the mountain year.

Elevation is only one contributor to diversity. Equally significant are differences in habitats caused by variations in available moisture. Where soil is kept wet throughout the summer by creeks or springs, green meadows and bogs and marshes glow bright with greedy-drinking flowers. In striking contrast are such places as Pumice Desert, where the sky supplies precipitation a-plenty but porous soils quickly drain it away, creating near-desert conditions, the scattered blossoms of tough, water-thrifty species seeming miracles amid sterile wastes of volcanic ash. And on high-country lava buttresses, where hot sunshine alternates with cold winds, scorching days with dewy-misty nights, the rock gardens drive to despair green-thumbers recalling their yards at home.

Fruiting head of western pasqueflower

Lyall lupine

Scarlet gilia

Bleeding heart

Paintbrush

Sulphur-flower

Rabbitbrush

Dirty socks

Left: Lewis monkeyflower

Tour boat on Crater Lake

LAKE SHORE

To view Crater Lake from the caldera rim is to know only the half of it. For the full experience one must go down to the water, descending the 1.1-mile Cleetwood Cove Trail (named for the geologists' boat of 1886) a steep 674 feet to the shore. There the visitor may pay the fare and board a passenger launch and circle the lake, passing under cliffs, into coves, around points, by Phantom Ship and Wizard Island — where the moderately ambitious can debark for the 1.2-mile hike to the summit, returning later in the day on another launch.

The lake has no known outlet. Because evaporation and seepage balance precipitation, the level is virtually constant at 6176 feet above sealevel, rarely varying more than 3 feet during the year. The maxi- mum known elevation of the surface was 6180.5 feet, a fact deter- mined by studies of crustose lichen made between 1916 and 1960; that stage may have occurred near the close of the 19th century. The presence of living pine trees slightly higher suggest the lake has not been materially higher for several centuries, if ever.

From a boat one can best observe the extraordinary clarity of the water and variegated hues of rough cliffs, and also gain deeper insights into Mt. Mazama's past. The green bands of plants on slopes of naked rock mark springs seeping from glacial debris enlayered between lava flows and pumice deposits, evidence of the repeated alternations over the eons of fire and ice. And the U shapes of Sun and Kerr Notches in the rim speak eloquently of Llao's end, of the glacier troughs and glaciers and mountain all destroyed that horrid week of not so long ago.

AUTO TOURS

The 33-mile Rim Drive encircling the caldera, usually open from mid-July to mid-October, can be done in little more than an hour, but shouldn't be. To pause at turnouts to savor the succession of changing views, and to sample the trails, a full day is essential — or several.

A 6-mile side-road leads from Kerr Notch down Sand Creek to The Pinnacles, 200-foot spires of pumice and tuff. Many are hollow, the gas vents still open.

A 4-mile, one-way "motor nature trail," narrow and winding and low-speed, traverses Grayback Ridge, permitting close and leisurely sit-down enjoyment of trees and flowers and volcanic rocks.

Two loop drives starting and ending outside the park broaden comprehension of the Crater Lake region. Either can be done in an easy day.

To best experience forests, take the loop from Medford to the north entrance of the park, thence to the west entrance, and back to Medford. Plan to linger more than a little while in superb trees of the Rogue River valley.

To best "see" Llao's mountain as the Ouxkanee did, take the loop from US 97 to the north entrance, thence to the south entrance, and back to US 97. The semi-desert allows views unobstructed by trees. A roadside exhibit near Fort Klamath superimposes the shape of old Mt. Mazama on a photograph of the existing skyline; one cannot help but gasp.

The Pinnacles

Overleaf: Sunrise on Crater Lake and Wizard Island

WINTER

Another season, another world. Simple, austere. Some 50 feet of snow are dumped on Crater Lake in the average winter, and winds blow cold and lava cliffs are ice-glazed and dwarfed trees become sculptures in hoarfrost. And when the low sun breaks free from storm clouds the never-frozen lake turns in a flash from dull gray to a blue far brighter than ever is seen in summer, and Mt. Mazama's companion volcanoes north and south seem to grow taller, brilliant-gleaming high above valley greens and desert browns.

The park's south and west entrance roads are plowed all winter to Rim Village; during midwinter chains are usually required on the last 3 miles. The sole civilized amenity is the coffee shop, open daily as a refuge from the chill.

Most winter visitors are content with a quick look at the lake from the parking lot, perhaps a snowball fight, a hot cup of coffee, and a descent to less stimulating climes.

Others don snowshoes or cross-country skis, parkas and mittens and goggles, and stride into the white wilderness for a day of peace beyond machines. A few load their backs with tents, sleeping bags, stoves, and food; miles from coffee shop and very very far from summer crowds they achieve the most mystic of experiences possible in the ruins of Llao's mountain, a winter night on the caldera rim.

Garfield Peak and snowdrifts banked against Crater Lake Lodge

Clark's nutcracker

Crater Lake highway and Ponderosa pines

Western grebe

KLAMATH BASIN NATIONAL WILDLIFE REFUGES

When it was the land of the Ouxkanee, the million-acre Klamath Basin contained a vast expanse of lakes and marshes ideal for waterfowl courtship and nesting. Moreover, so abundant was feed and undisturbed habitat that tremendous flocks of ducks and geese paused for recuperation on journeys north in spring and south in fall; whether following the seacoast or the inland route, 70-80 percent of waterfowl migrating on the Pacific Flyway veered east or west to funnel through the basin.

But white settlers saw that if wetlands were drained the rich soils would yield bonanza harvests, as would sagebrush flats if irrigated. Soon virtually the whole basin was being converted to agriculture.

As examples of the drastic changes, Tule Lake was reduced from almost 100,000 to 13,000 acres; Clear Lake was emptied entirely and remained dry from 1921 to 1942. There was even a scheme to tap Crater Lake for irrigation water!

The numbers of nesting birds declined sharply, some species nearly disappearing. Migratory fowl, continuing to fly ancestral routes and finding natural feed diminished, accepted the substitute unwillingly provided by farmers, who in frustration and fury mounted campaigns to gang-slaughter the "pests." One of the world's great bird populations was in danger.

To the rescue in the nick of time came the emerging conservation ethic; beginning in 1908 portions of Klamath Basin were set aside as wildlife refuges, secure from further encroachment. The first, the

Lower Klamath Refuge, now consists of 21,500 acres of lake, marsh, and upland. In 1911 was established the Clear Lake Refuge of 33,400 acres, the now partly-refilled lake surrounded by sagebrush. Tule Lake Refuge, dating from 1928, is 37,300 acres. In the same year was created the 12,700-acre Upper Klamath Refuge in shallows of Upper Klamath Lake, unique for its huge tule marsh. Finally, in 1958 the 15,200-acre Klamath Forest Refuge was acquired.

Though their domain is much smaller than formerly, birds crowd enthusiastically into what remains. To maintain habitats, the U.S. Fish and Wildlife Service, the wildlife manager, buys water (that otherwise would be used for irrigation) from the principal land manager, the Bureau of Reclamation. Grain is planted on the refuges to compensate for the loss of natural feed. Though far different from the era of the Ouxkanee, conditions are such that the surviving population is relatively safe. Many species once almost gone are slowly being restored.

Because of the diversity — lakes and marshes, grassy meadows and farms, sagebrush and junipers, lava flows and coniferous forests — few areas anywhere offer comparable opportunities for viewing waterfowl, marsh birds, shore birds, upland birds. Some 275 species have been recorded on the refuges; 180 species regularly nest.

From spring through summer, particularly in July and August, the visitor sees countless broods of young fowl swimming in open waters, feeding on shores. But the migrations are the mind-bogglers. In spring during early March, and especially in fall from October through early November, the sky literally darkens with wings. In the fall climax as many as 7 million birds (that count being made in 1955) have been concentrated in the refuges at a single time — of ducks, some 2 million pintails, 1 million ruddies, 300,000 mallards, 300,000 shovelers, 200,000 widgeons; of geese, 300,000 whitefronted, 300,000 cackling, 200,000 snow, and 5,000 Canada. And more, incredibly many more. Truly, the spectacle must be seen, and heard, to be believed.

Adult male white pelican

Double-crested cormorant

Egret

White pelicans

Pintails

American avocet

Right: Canada goose

Overleaf: Spring migration of snow geese at Tule Lake

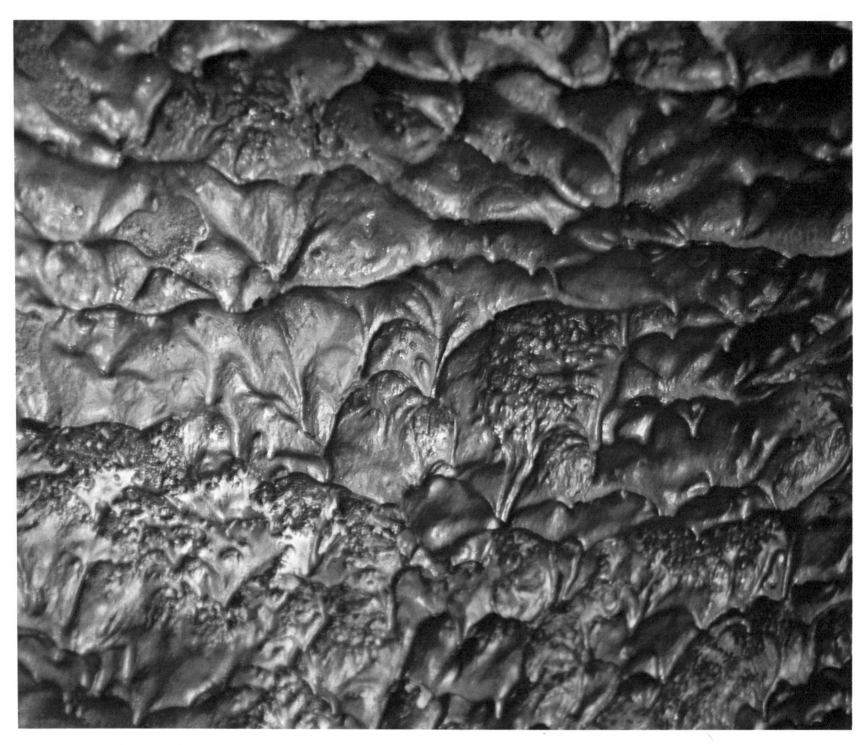

Lavacicles on the ceiling of Mush Pot Cave

Cleft in lava flow at Captain Jack's Stronghold. Mt. Shasta in distance

LAVA BEDS NATIONAL MONUMENT

A raw land only just created, scene of some of the most recent volcanic activity in the Northwest. Battlefields of the sole major Indian war fought in California. To encompass these was established in 1925 the 72-square-mile Lava Beds National Monument.

As scarcely needs be said, displays of the past's flaming violence are a central attraction. Not too many thousand years ago volcanoes poured out great streams and sheets of basaltic lava, both relatively smooth pahoehoe and rougher aa. Within them are numerous lava-tube caves formed by the surface cooling and hardening while still-liquid rock flowed from under; 19 are open for exploration on the "cave loop" trail behind the monument headquarters, including several that retain winter's ice all the long hot summer; in the monument as a whole are some 300 caves. Scattered over the forbidding world-dawn plateau are dozens of cinder and spatter cones.

Equally imagination-stirring are memories of the Modoc War of 1872. The Indians, pushed off their lands by settlers, at last struck back in despair. Led by "Captain Jack," a small band then retreated into the desolate lava and for 6 months repulsed attacks by vastly superior numbers of federal and volunteer troops. In the end, of course, they lost the war, their lands, and their tribal existence. Modoc and troop positions can be inspected at Captain Jack's Stronghold and other battlegrounds.

A system of roads and short trails leads to points of volcanic and military interest. The more rugged — and properly equipped — visitor may set forth on longer trails penetrating the wilderness portion of the monument, hiking through desert grasslands and sagebrush, belts of juniper and chaparral, into Ponderosa pine forests at higher elevations. Because guns are banned, chances are good to see wildlife — chipmunks and squirrels, rattlesnakes and jackrabbits, owls and hawks and eagles. Winter is the best time for encountering deer and coyote, summer for antelope and bighorn sheep, perhaps bobcat, maybe even a cougar.

Entrance to Skull Cave, Lava Beds National Monument

Rift in lava used by Captain Jack

Overleaf: Snow-plastered trees on caldera rim. Mt. Scott in distance

REDWOOD

NATIONAL PARK

and
Jedediah Smith Redwoods
State Park

Del Norte Coast Redwoods
State Park

Prairie Creek Redwoods
State Park

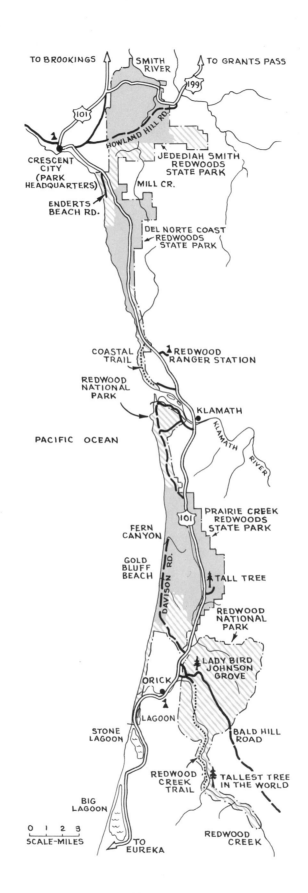

TO BROOKINGS   SMITH RIVER   TO GRANTS PASS

199

101

HOWLAND HILL RD.

CRESCENT CITY (PARK HEADQUARTERS)

JEDEDIAH SMITH REDWOODS STATE PARK

MILL CR.

ENDERTS BEACH RD.

DEL NORTE COAST REDWOODS STATE PARK

COASTAL TRAIL   REDWOOD RANGER STATION

REDWOOD NATIONAL PARK

KLAMATH

KLAMATH RIVER

PACIFIC OCEAN

PRAIRIE CREEK REDWOODS STATE PARK

101

FERN CANYON

GOLD BLUFF BEACH

DAVISON RD.

TALL TREE

REDWOOD NATIONAL PARK

LADY BIRD JOHNSON GROVE

ORICK

LAGOON

STONE LAGOON

BALD HILL ROAD

REDWOOD CREEK TRAIL   TALLEST TREE IN THE WORLD

BIG LAGOON

0 1 2 3
SCALE-MILES

TO EUREKA

REDWOOD CREEK

Previous page: Rhododendrons in redwood forest

REDWOOD NATIONAL PARK

Fog fills the forest, muting the babble of a creek, the song of a wren. From massed green ferns the rough-barked trunks rise high, and higher, dimming in gray mist to a black tracery of delicate, feather-like foliage. Far, far above the trail the crowns of the trees intermesh in a canopy so dense the sky is more guessed than seen.

Too much awed, too much humbled, a visitor may escape to the freedom of ocean horizons, to bright rays piercing the fog. Yet as sun nears the sea and lingering clouds blaze orange and scarlet, the pounding surf again reminds of his smallness. Not for the egotist is redwood country, neither forest nor beach.

In warm and humid Cretaceous times, 130 million years ago, redwood ancestors thrived around the planet, even north of the Arctic Circle. Before the advance of cold and dry glacial air, beginning 58 million years ago, the redwood steadily retreated, eventually losing the whole of its dominions except a province of China and parts of California, and all its species except three—a *metasequoia* in China and the two species in California which have been called "the last of the true sequoias, a living link to the age of the dinosaurs."

Sequoiadendron giganteum, variously called giant sequoia, big tree, and Sierra redwood, lives at elevations from 4000-8000 feet in the Sierra Nevada, attaining ages of more than 4000 years. The General Sherman is the world's largest tree, 272 feet in height, 32 feet in diameter.

Sequoia sempervirens, the coast redwood, lives "only" to some 2200 years, grows "only" to diameters of some 20 feet, but is surpassed in bulk by none but its Sierra cousin. Coast redwoods are the world's tallest trees, heights of 300 feet common, 367.8 feet the record.

The last natural stand on Earth of *Sequoia sempervirens* is a belt 5-35 miles wide and 450 miles long, from the Santa Lucia Mountains to just barely into Oregon. Why here, and solely here?

To dominate competitors—indeed, to survive among them—the tree requires mild temperatures and heavy rainfall; in the national park the mean annual temperature is 50°-60°F, the precipitation 80-100 inches. Above all it demands crown-bathing mists; the natural range is restricted to the realm of frequent summer fogs. In nature, as distinguished from man-tended gardens and arboretums, the one remaining place providing the precise necessary conditions is the northern California coast.

Though redwoods grow from sealevel to 3000 feet, at the higher altitudes they yield to Douglas fir, madrone, and tan oak, and at the storm-blasted ocean edge to Sitka spruce. The climax magnificence is displayed on river flats and gentle hillsides below 1000 feet. On these choice sites the tree's photosynthesis is so incredibly efficient it can achieve a height of 100-150 feet in 50 years. Once reaching the canopy, the trees may survive 500 to 1500 years before dying. The oldest known coast redwood was more than 2200 years old when cut.

In 1847 the Hungarian botanist, Stephen Endlicher, named the genus *Sequoia* (for the famous Cherokee alphabet inventor, in whose native language the word means "opossum") and the species *sempervirens* (evergreen). At that time redwood forests, defined as forests where 20 percent or more of the trees are redwoods, covered an area variously estimated as from 1,586,000 to 1,918,000 acres. By 1885 all had slipped from public to private ownership and logging was underway—and continues today in the perhaps 9 percent of essentially untouched virgin forests left as of late 1974.

Of that 9 percent, approximately two-thirds is owned by timber companies, which are logging, according to one guess, some 10,000 acres a year. The companies now replant cutover areas, planning to harvest the next crop in 50-odd years. At that age "farm" redwoods may be very big, very valuable, very beautiful. A "cathedral" forest, however, is not built in less than 500-800 years.

Even during the frontier era a handful of people recognized the difference between a farm and a cathedral, and man's need for both. In 1890 samples of the giant sequoia were preserved in national parks. The coast redwood had to wait. Since 1918 the Save-the-Redwoods League has solicited contributions to purchase private lands. Through its efforts, supplemented by government actions, groves have been protected in 25 California state parks.

Protected? Starting in 1955 catastrophic floods of Bull Creek, in Humboldt Redwoods State Park, destroyed 900 "saved" giants of world-renowned Rockefeller Grove. Scientists found that due mainly to clearcut logging, erosion of fragile and unstable soils on steep slopes of the redwood region had increased to 50 times the natural rate. They declared that to genuinely protect the virgin forest it was necessary to preserve not mere groves but entire watershed ecosystems.

No park proposal ever has triggered a greater explosion of letters, pro and con, than the one that culminated in the compromise legislation signed into law by President Lyndon B. Johnson on October 2, 1968, establishing Redwood National Park. Far smaller than the 90,000 acres proponents sought, and still not encompassing complete watersheds, the park is authorized for an ultimate size of 58,000 acres, which includes 28,280 acres of formerly private land, plus (if and when donated) the 27,468 acres of three state parks created in the 1920s—Prairie Creek, Del Norte Coast, and Jedediah Smith.

James Irvine Trail

FERNS

In twilight depths of the pure and ancient redwood forest the great trees stand amid endless green seas of ferns.

Far and away most common is the exuberant sword fern. Many a trail trenches for miles through massed fronds as high as a hiker's hips.

Where creeks slice deep gorges, as in Fern Canyon, vertical walls rising from the rushing water are covered with tapestries of five-fingered fern.

In other dark, moist corners of the forest are generous sprinklings of lady fern, wood fern, deer fern, and maidenhair. Also to be found are the bladder, gold, licorice, and chain ferns, and on open hillsides, the bracken.

From a car a visitor glimpses ferns. To become immersed in their green mystery, though, he must leave roads, must follow paths into forests and along streams.

Licorice fern   *Sword fern*   *Deer fern*

Five-fingered fern in Fern Canyon

Sunburst in fog-shrouded redwood forest

Rhododendron bud

Stout Tree, 20 feet in diameter and 340 feet high

Vanilla leaf

Two-leaved Solomon's Seal

Iris

Salal

Salmonberry

FLOWERS OF THE FOREST

Though the redwood lords it over the community, a myriad other plants enrich the lush understory and groundcover.

Douglas fir shares the canopy with the redwood. Coniferous trees of lesser stature include hemlock, grand fir, and Port Orford cedar. Among understory hardwoods are tan oak and madrone, abundant at higher elevations; chinquapin, laurel, wax myrtle, ash, and cascara; alders and willows and maples.

There are shrubs, low-growing or nearly tree-size: deer brush, hazel, salal, Oregon grape, rhododendron, azalea, and honeysuckle; and the berries—thimble, salmon, black, Himalaya, huckle, elder, goose, and currant. And a dozen ferns, innumerable fungi and mosses and lichens, and hundreds of herbs.

Hardly a week of the year does not have, somewhere, a display, glorious or modest, of flowering shrubs and herbs. Spring and early summer, of course, are the prime show time. Star attractions of March are the violet and coltsfoot and red currant. April brings the blooming of the trillium, false Solomon's seal, fairybells, and the many-acred carpets of oxalis. May and June offer the magnificence of rhododendron pink spiced by azalea white, and, if the visitor pokes aside its leaves, the elusive blossom of the wild ginger. In midsummer the orange tiger lily grows along roads, the yellow mimulus by creeks.

In proper season, in the proper spots, there is more magic, evoked by names: star flower, anemone, milkmaid, bleeding heart, fairy lantern, sugar scoop, inside-out flower, heart's ease, ocean spray, sweet Cicely. Nor can one ignore the skunk cabbage.

Oxalis

Tiger lily

Fern Canyon and Home Creek

Tall Tree Grove

Tallest known tree in the world

TRAILS

Highways and side-roads provide views of forest and ocean as good or better than any on the trails. But the trails are more peaceful. And somehow a view seems finer when attained in the natural, non-mechanized manner.

Nooks and crannies of the park area are probed by 30 trails totalling over 100 miles. Some are thronged, others lonesome. Some require merely a leisurely hour, others can fill a long, rich day, and one is best done as an overnight backpack. For a full listing consult maps issued at information offices, or ask the rangers, who always are happy to share their favorite walks. (But not with pets, which are banned from trails.)

Redwood Creek near Tall Tree Grove

Among the short paths are self-guiding nature trails with brochures keyed to points of interest on the way. The Revelation Trail is designed for the blind as well as the sighted, a wood-and-rope hand-railing running the ¼-mile length, "touchable" features keyed by knots in the rope to a Braille guidebook.

Solitude is assured on many of the half-day or all-day tramps, notably the Rhododendron Trail. The James Irvine Trail goves over-land 4½ miles to Fern Canyon, and the Boy Scout Trail to a charming little waterfall. The 4-mile Coastal Trail from Requa to False Klamath Cove wanders along grassy hillsides and through spruce forests, out on bluffs offering broad ocean panoramas.

The Redwood Creek Trail leads in 8 miles to the world's tallest known trees. Though the round-trip can be done in a day, most hikers carry overnight gear and camp on a friendly gravel bar.

When measured in 1963 by the National Geographic Society, the Tall Tree was approximately 600 years old and was 367.8 feet tall and 14 feet in diameter. The top 15 feet or so are dead and should part of this section break off during a high wind, the title would pass to the second-tallest tree, a half-mile down the creek. (The third- and sixth-tallest trees also are in the national park.)

The future of the Tall Tree Grove is in doubt. Though in the lower Redwood Creek valley the park bulges out to extend from ridgetop to ridgetop, upstream the boundary comes within a quarter-mile of the creek on both sides and at several points logging is in sight or sound from the trail. Outside the park the bulk of the valley already has been clearcut or will be by 1980 or so. The big question is: has Redwood Creek been destabilized and will it follow the example of Bull Creek?

Overleaf: Rhododendrons blooming in redwood forest

Raccoon feeding on tideflat near mouth of the Klamath River

ANIMALS OF THE LAND

A visitor walking through meadows and along margins of the deep forest frequently encounters slithering garter snakes, croaking frogs, and gaudy banana slugs, sometimes chattering squirrels and chipmunks, occasionally a salamander or newt. If sufficiently patient he may glimpse a member of the beaver colony living in clay banks near the mouth of the Klamath River, or if very lucky, a river otter at play. By staying awake all night, listening, flashlight handy, he might surprise creatures of nocturnal habits—the raccoon, skunk, mountain beaver, porcupine, mouse, and rat. Rarely will he see the deer and bear and coyote, the fox and cougar and bobcat.

The largest of the resident animals, the Roosevelt elk, he is almost certain to meet. Several bands, containing virtually the whole of California's surviving elk population, are found near Orick. Two of the largest headquarter in Prairie Creek Redwoods State Park. Morning and evening, one band generally is in a meadow beside the Redwood Highway, the other somewhere near Gold Bluff Beach.

These elk are unafraid of humans and thus dangerous to approach. When annoyed they normally run off—but may charge, and pawing hooves of the cows are as frightening as antlers of the bulls, particularly during the fall rutting season. The safest observations are from within cars.

Roosevelt elk grazing near the Gold Bluff Beach road

Steller sea lions

Hidden Beach

Strawberry

Ice-plant

Beach morning-glory

Hen-and-chicks

Cow parsnip

Poison oak

PLANTS OF THE BEACH

Were a visitor to walk from a summit of the Coast Range to the sea, he might pass through as many as a score of strikingly diverse eco-systems. Traveling by land, he would descend from the high chaparral into a succession of several quite different types of forest, ending on scrub-covered bluffs dropping steeply to the shore. If he chose an all-water route, his journey would be enriched by life systems of river and estuary, marshes and lagoons, some enclosed by spits topped by sand dunes. And finally the beach.

Assume, though, the visitor lacks time for the complete traverse, has only an afternoon to spare, and that for the concluding segment.

Walking westward he leaves the redwood, which cannot take the brunt of storm winds and salt spray, and enters Sitka spruce, which can. Yet even for this tough tree existence is a struggle on slopes facing the ocean. Buffeted by winter gales, windward buds damaged by blowing salt, misshapened and distorted, the spruce is sculptured into grotesque forms, the more picturesque for the "old man's beard" of lichen draping the branches.

Along the coast may be thickets of a shrub with clusters of three shiny leaves. Poison oak! To avoid a rash the visitor stays clear of the evil plant—but in autumn rejoices in its rioting color.

On open hillsides overlooking the surf are communities of iris, lupine, columbine, and Indian paintbrush, clumps of coyote brush, silk tassel, and sagebrush-like artemisia, and cow parsnip growing to heights of 6 feet and more.

Scrambling to the foot of the bluff and the adjoining ribbon of beach above normal high tides, the visitor finds a simple, stark community adapted to the harshness of sand, strong winds, extremes of heat and cold, and occasional invasions by storm-driven breakers. Here is a palette rivalling that of alpine meadows—the purple blossoms of morning-glory and evening primroses, the yellow of golden rod and sand verbena, and the white of strawberry, daisy, knot-weed, ice-plant, and sea foam.

Another few steps and the sparse grasses, the startling blooms of sea rocket, mark the farthest reach of plants of the land, the beginning of sterile sand, beyond which grow the plants of the sea.

ANIMALS OF THE SEA

In tidepools below rocky headlands lives a community of plants and animals that seems indestructible, withstanding as it does the pounding of Pacific storms. Yet it has not been tough enough to survive Man the Collector. Over past decades souvenir hunters and students in biology classes stripped tidepools bare. Now, protected by state law, marine life is slowly rebuilding. The visitor should explore the pools within the park at low tide and (being careful of slippery rocks and surging waves) observe, enjoy—*but not touch*—sea urchins, starfish, and sea anemones.

That mammals should inhabit the ocean never fails to surprise. Among the most delightful of wildlife encounters is to be walking a beach and find oneself accompanied by a harbor seal, constantly popping its head in and out of the surf, as astonished by this two-legged mammal walking the land as the walker is by this two-flippered mammal swimming the sea.

Harbor seals are rather dog-like in size and curiosity. Sea lions are far larger, up to 2000 pounds for a male, and utterly lacking any taste for human company. Chances for close-up study thus are rare, the best perhaps coming in spring, when they may be seen fishing several miles up the Klamath River.

Distant views, aided by binoculars, are more common. Castle Island, opposite Crescent City, is home sweet home to a large colony of sea lions. From May through July they also come ashore on one very isolated beach below the Coastal Trail to sleep in the sun, their privacy guarded by a near-vertical cliff covered with poison oak. However, the trail skirts the top of the bluff above the beach and from this respectful distance a hiker can look down upon the snoozing beasts. The racket they make yelling at each other can be heard a mile away at the Requa parking lot.

Requiring a trained eye to identify are the dolphins and porpoises that cavort offshore. Killer whales, though, sometimes feed in shallow waters, occasionally within a hundred yards of the beach.

What animal provides the biggest thrill? The biggest, of course. During spring and fall migrations gray whales swim along the coast; a few stragglers pass by in summer. From a viewpoint on a bluff a visitor may see a plume of spray, then a fin and tail as the monster dives. Once in a great while a dead whale is washed ashore; only on such sad occasions can one grasp the size of these mammals, up to 50 feet in length, weighing as much as 35 tons.

Scene along the Coastal Trail

Tidepool with sea anemone and starfish

Mouth of Klamath River from south end of Coastal Trail on Requa Hill

BIRDS

In the redwood forest wrens and sparrows and warblers flit through shadows, robins and varied thrushes sing in glades, here and there woodpeckers rat-a-tat-tat and Steller's jays squawk, and at night owls hoot. Far busier are airways of the meadows, lively with swallows and juncos and chickadees and hummingbirds. Along creeks a visitor almost always sees water ouzels and sandpipers, and on rivers kingfishers and osprey and mergansers.

The devout birdwatcher does best, though, to head for the beach. Little turnstones bob up and down, digging out sand fleas. Black oystercatchers probe mussel beds with brilliant orange bills. Everywhere are sea gulls riding the wind.

Often viewed on tide flats, in tidepools, and anywhere along the coast near lagoons and creeks, is the great blue heron, typically standing motionless, waiting to grab a dinner with its long sharp bill. Herons regularly fish Lagoon Creek, especially after the game department has stocked the waters, but are extremely shy and fly away if approached.

From the Yurok Loop Trail in summer thousands of nesting birds can be seen on offshore rocks, mainly the jet-black cormorant and penguin-like murre. During spring and fall migrations many species of ducks and geese fly in formation overhead, sometimes descending to rivers and lagoons for rest and feed.

The favorite of most visitors is the brown pelican, a big-beaked bird that looks much too awkward to fly. The more surprising, then, when with several flaps of large wings it abruptly takes off to soar gracefully over the sea and, upon spotting a fish, plummets headfirst into the water. A colony of brown pelicans summers in redwood country; they are seen all along the coast and in harbors and the mouths of creeks and rivers.

Blue heron

Blue heron's tracks

Cormorants

Sea gulls

178

Brown pelicans

Brown pelican fishing near the mouth of the Klamath River

Battery Point Lighthouse at Crescent City

Sunset from Yurok Loop Trail

Clam digging on South Beach, Crescent City

EXPLORING REDWOOD COUNTRY

The average visitor is unaware whether he is in a state park or the present national park. But each is administered by a separate agency with its own facilities and regulations. Together they occupy an area extending 46 north-south miles and, at the widest, 7 miles up valleys of the Coast Range. From U.S. Highways 101 and 199, from half a dozen narrow, low-speed side-roads, from a hundred miles of trails, one can savor the coast redwoods and sea, can ponder past eons, can wonder about future decades.

Convenient bases for exploration are provided by campgrounds in the three state parks (in summer be sure to make reservations) and adjoining Six Rivers National Forest and by private accommodations. Excellent preparations for independent wanderings are the evening programs offered in summer at various park locations and the beach and forest hikes led by ranger-naturalists.

There is much else besides park forests and beaches to see in the area: on a free sawmill tour, the transformation of redwoods into lumber; plantations of young trees in an industry-sponsored demonstration forest; in late summer, when salmon arrive to spawn, hundreds of sport fishermen's boats gunwale to gunwale in the Klamath River, plus a Coast Guard boat standing by to rescue anyone washed out to sea; commercial fishing boats unloading in Crescent City harbor; the Lighthouse Museum; the inland Klamath River, on a 32-mile cruise upstream.

Most visitors know only the redwoods of summer, the mood of foggy mornings and partly-sunny afternoons. Many, intrigued, return in other seasons to feel other moods: in spring, the brisk, clear days and the blossoming of the flowers; in fall, the brilliant yellows and reds of maples; in winter, the drenching storms and the wet dim silence of the cathedral groves.

Driftwood on Wilson Creek Beach

Lupine at False Klamath Cove